GUYANA
IN THE
SHADOWS OF THE
AMAZON

GUYANA
IN THE
SHADOWS OF THE
AMAZON

RABINDRA N PRASAD
AKA "TAZ"

GUYANA – In The Shadows of the Amazon

HOV Publishing is a division of HOV, LLC.
email: hopeofvision@gmail.com
www.hovpub.com

Front Cover Illustration: Ariana Dharambeer
Cover Design: HOV Design Solutions
Interior Text: HOV Design Solutions
Photo Credits: Rabindra N Prasad
Editing: HOV Publishing Editing Team

ISBN Paperback: 978-1-955107-06-8
ISBN Hardcase: 978-1-955107-05-1
ISBN eBook: 978-1-955107-04-4

Printed in the United States of America

DEDICATION

Sam and Kusil Moorley gave me the opportunity
to be who I am.

ACKNOWLEDGMENTS

Ronnie Oddo, District Manager

Edgar Reyes

Satish S. Wilfred, Store Manager

Wendell Cunningham, Asst. Store Manager

Janet Nelson

Wilfred

Miss Diana

My Home Depot encouragement group that never fails to point out the bright horizon of accomplishment.

To all of them, my Special Thanks.

Special Acknowledgment

A heartfelt thank you to Ariana Dharambeer, my beloved granddaughter, for her brilliant work as the front cover illustrator of Guyana In The Shadows of the Amazon.

With deep understanding and artistic sensitivity, Ariana captured not only the visual essence but also the emotional spirit of the story. Her vision brought to life the landscapes, mysteries, and energy of the Guyanese coast in a way only someone so close to my heart could achieve.

TABLE OF CONTENTS

INTRODUCTION

In the Beginning

The origins of this narrative stem from manuscripts I penned more than three decades ago, drawn from multiple retellings by the native guides who accompanied me on my journeys. Their stories, passed down through generations, were sometimes reluctant to surface, requiring gentle coaxing—sometimes with a sip of strong spirits—to loosen the threads of memory. Occasionally, they needed reminders to pick up where they had left off, leading them to restart their tales from the beginning. It was through these repeated telling's that the narrative took shape, lending itself to a sequence that, while sometimes disjointed, captures the essence of the lived experiences of the people and the land.

The wild coast of northern South America—home to pioneering settlements shaped by European colonial ambitions—was a battleground of warring empires. The rivalry between European powers extended beyond the continent, spilling into their colonial holdings, where success often hinged on brute force, cunning, and piracy. Monarchs, eager for a share of the spoils, encouraged the plundering of rival plantations.

The Dutch West India Company commanded fleets of shallow-draft vessels designed for commerce, exchanging European manufactured goods and tools for colonial produce: gold, precious stones, wild honey, dried and fresh meat, fish, animal skins, cotton, sugar, and commodities such as cocoa and coffee—valuable currencies of the colonial world. Piracy thrived, both as a deliberate enterprise and through opportunistic raids, mirroring the chaos of the eastern Caribbean.

One such event involved *The Vlessen*, a vessel of the Dutch West India Company. While anchored at a settlement near the estuary of the Corentyne River, Captain Jan John and his 80-man crew received intelligence about prosperous plantations along the infamous Devil's Creek. Tales spoke of hidden stores of gold, precious stones, and hogsheads of sugar, rum, and molasses, all awaiting shipment to Europe. The plantation, heavily reliant on enslaved labor under French control, was said to be ripe for the taking.

Under the cover of darkness, *The Vlessen* dropped anchor in the tar-black waters of Devil's Creek, roughly ten miles from the Berbice River. The moon would not rise for another four hours, providing a perfect opportunity for an ambush. Captain Jan John addressed his lieutenants in hushed tones:

"Speed, surprise, and silence are our greatest advantages tonight. Go and take what is ours."

Two longboats were lowered into the still waters, and forty cutthroats descended by rope ladders. The raiders, divided into two groups of twenty, paddled quietly through the creek, avoiding the use of oars to maintain stealth. The waters of Devil's Creek, fed by the vast silicate-white sands of the inland mountains, carried a swift undercurrent, swelled further by seasonal rains. Dense aquatic weeds blanketed the surface, obscuring their passage.

The jungle was alive with sound—shrieking hawks feasting on large bats, the splashes of predatory tarpons and lurking caimans, the symphony of bullfrogs and rustling leaves. As the boats glided forward, a long viper, its head poised above the water, drifted effortlessly across their path. The men, seasoned but wary, tensed at the sudden movements of a startled flock of *caryie* pheasants erupting from their nests.

"Steady!" whispered one of the overseers. "Likely a water snake… perhaps a young anaconda hunting for eggs."

As dawn crept closer, their eyes adjusted to the dim starlight. The lead overseer signaled the boats to veer toward an overhanging cotton tree on the creek's western bank.

"We're two leagues from the plantation. We move in single file, absolute silence. No sudden noises. Don't even swat a mosquito," he hissed.

At the plantation, the attack was swift and precise. The pirates divided into pre-arranged groups: one to subdue the slave barracks, another to seize the storage warehouses, and the most daring to capture the manager's mansion. The first guard, drowsy at his post, barely had time to register the cold steel against his throat before he was silenced.

The pirates scaled the stilts of the main house, bursting into rooms and tying up the terrified occupants with minimal resistance.

By moonlight, the captives—European plantation managers and shareholders—were bound and gagged in the compound's center. They were beaten and tortured for their valuables, their European, native, and enslaved women subjected to unspeakable fates. Six plantation boats were commandeered, and the vast stores of sugar, rum, tobacco, dried fish, and honey were ferried back to *The Vlessen*. Twenty skilled enslaved laborers—carpenters, interpreters, and foragers—were forcibly recruited into the pirate ranks.

As dawn broke, *The Vlessen* set sail from Devil's Creek, merging into the Berbice River estuary. Overhead, storm clouds loomed—dark omens of the turbulent waters ahead.

Meanwhile, far to the south, the Spanish galleon *La Tormenta*—laden with Peruvian gold and colonial riches—made her way around Cape Horn, bound for the Orinoco River settlements. Caught in a violent storm, she was driven off course, running around on the mudbanks of the Essequibo River estuary. With a sixty-degree list, her forty cannons lay buried in the mud, while those on the starboard side pointed uselessly at the sky. Seawater seeped into her hull as the tide rose, sealing her fate.

It was *The Vlessen* that first spotted the stranded galleon. Seizing the opportunity, Captain Jan John ordered an assault. The Dutch pirates swarmed *La Tormenta*, toppling her masts and rendering her immobile.

"Into the longboats! Take only the essentials—food, weapons, and gold!"

Captain Pedro Cadiz of *La Tormenta* and his crew had little choice but to abandon ship. Overwhelmed by greed, the Dutch raiders focused on plundering the galleon's wealth, ignoring the escaping Spanish sailors and passengers who vanished into the jungle.

The haul was unprecedented: bales of cotton, hogsheads of sugar, barrels of rum and molasses, crates of dried fish, and casks of gunpowder and muskets. The greatest prize lay in the captain's quarters—two chests filled with gold bars, native artifacts, and a treasure trove of silver bullion. In the cargo hold, the most valuable item of all—a solid gold throne intended for a European monarch—was carefully hoisted onto *The Vlessen*.

Thus, the brutal cycle of piracy continued, century after violent century, along the treacherous waters of the Guiana Shield. Some raids were criminal enterprises driven by greed, others acts of vengeance or jealousy. Many remain unsolved mysteries, woven into the relentless struggle for power and control over these contested lands.

CHAPTER 1

The Early Colonization of Guyana

In the early seventeenth century, the northern coast of South America, stretching from the Orinoco River to the Tumuc-Humac mountains along the Atlantic Ocean, was known as Guyana. European explorers from England, Holland, France, and Portugal attempted to establish settlements along this approximately twelve to fifteen hundred-mile stretch of fertile jungle and swamp land.

In 1616, Sir Walter Raleigh of England led an expedition up the Essequibo River to locate the legendary city of gold, El Dorado. However, the harsh jungles and swamps of the interior humbled Raleigh's team. Returning to England as a failure, Raleigh was executed in disgrace, partly due to his previous conviction, which was revived by the humiliation of his unsuccessful venture. No gold was ever found, despite Raleigh's confident boasts that he would uncover this illustrious city, which he claimed would greatly enrich the English treasury.

In 1627, the Dutch explorer and colonizer Abraham Van Peere established a settlement on the east bank of the Berbice River, naming it New Amsterdam, reminiscent of Holland. Later, King Charles II of England granted land to Lord Willoughby and Lawrence Hyde in 1650 to establish a colony eighty miles from the eastern bank of the Corentyne

River, near the Coppermine River. Consequently, the region of Suriname initially became British territory, while Berbice remained Dutch.

Rivalries between European countries to seize lands in South America led to frequent changes in colonial rule. This, in turn, sparked the modern border disputes that plague these nations even after gaining independence. The colony of British Guyana was formed in 1831 by merging three separate colonies—Essequibo, Demerara, and Berbice—under a single administration. The eastern border of this new colony was left undefined, existing between the area granted to Lord Willoughby and Lawrence Hyde and the Corentyne River, an unclaimed and unsettled "no man's land."

The fertile lands along the Corentyne River's east and west banks were farmed for cotton, yielding remarkable success. English and Dutch entrepreneurs applied for plantation grants to cultivate sugar cane, a commodity in high demand in Europe. Cotton fueled the textile mills of the Industrial Revolution, while sugar sweetened coffee, cocoa, and tea, becoming an essential part of European diets.

Settlers on the east bank of the Corentyne sought grants from England or Holland, or sometimes from colonial representatives based at New Amsterdam. While the west bank was organized through legislative grants, "no man's land" on the east bank was settled by squatters. In 1875, near the confluence of the Corentyne and Nickerie Rivers, the settlement of New Rotterdam was established by a group of settlers including smugglers, rum runners, gold seekers, and balata bleeders. The Nickerie River's deep channel allowed small ocean-going vessels to dock, safe from the violent Atlantic storms. Manufactured goods were exchanged for raw materials from both Berbice and Suriname, creating a bustling port protected from pirate attacks common in the Caribbean Sea.

In 1879, New Rotterdam was devastated by a mini-hurricane and completely flooded. The settlement was moved about three miles inland along the Nickerie River bank, and new buildings were erected on higher ground. This new settlement, named New Nickerie, grew to boast a population of around eight thousand permanent residents by the early twentieth century, becoming the third most populous town in Suriname.

Around this time, the administration in Paramaribo moved to officially incorporate New Nickerie into Dutch territory. A market, bank, post office, two roads, a church, a makeshift hospital, a police station, and necessary trading offices marked its growth into a proper town. New Nickerie attracted residents from both Berbice and French Guiana, including freed slaves. In contrast to Berbice, where English influence dominated after the British regained control in the 1850s, New Nickerie's official language was a blend of Creole Dutch and English, known locally as "taki-taki."

Following the emancipation of slaves in British Guiana in 1838, most freed African slaves abandoned the sugar plantations, relocating to

Georgetown in Demerara, New Amsterdam in Berbice, and other towns. The British sought to replace the labor void of the liberated African slaves by importing Chinese and Portuguese workers, but these attempts failed due to the backbreaking nature of the work and the poor conditions, which proved fatal for many.

Next, the British turned to India, recruiting laborers from Uttar Pradesh and other states. Newspaper advertisements encouraged migration to British Guiana for a five-year period of indentured labor, promising riches and a return home with enough money to live comfortably. However, these advertisements painted a false picture, concealing the harsh realities awaiting the laborers. Many Indians signed up, driven by poverty, societal inequality, and a desire to escape India's rigid class system.

Once in British Guiana, indentured laborers faced brutal working conditions, often not much better than slavery. They were provided with poor housing, inadequate sanitation, and little access to healthcare. Swampy surroundings bred malaria, and makeshift treatments proved largely ineffective. Life on the Berbice cotton and sugar plantations was grueling, with workers laboring from sunrise to sunset for meager wages that barely covered necessities like food and clothing. Those who lost their jobs also lost their homes, as they were tied to the estates where they worked. Survival demanded adaptation; even vegetarian laborers turned to fishing and hunting for sustenance in the surrounding rivers and forests.

Fishing became a vital part of their subsistence. The rivers teemed with fish, crabs, and shrimp, which quickly became a dietary staple. As Berbice's population grew, so did the demand for marine-based protein. Small-scale farming could not keep up, and local boat builders experimented with native timbers like greenheart, cedar, and mora to construct seaworthy fishing boats. By the late nineteenth century, fishing boats powered by small diesel engines plied the waters off the coast of Berbice.

Meanwhile, Georgetown, the colony's capital, rapidly expanded. With limited educational facilities in the countryside, young people flocked to Georgetown for higher education and job opportunities, leading to a growing urban population. As Georgetown's outskirts developed into residential schemes, agricultural lands were converted into housing lots. The city thrived amidst a construction boom.

However, the political turmoil of the 1950s and 1960s culminated in Guyana gaining independence on February 23, 1966, under Prime Minister L.F.S. Burnham. Over the next two and a half decades, mismanagement, corruption, nepotism, and racial discrimination brought the country to the brink of bankruptcy. Import restrictions, coupled with dwindling foreign exchange reserves, left one of South America's most resource-rich nations in economic ruin.

CHAPTER 2

Paramaribo: A Colonial Capital's Rise

In the early stages of Northern Amazon colonization, the British established a foothold in Surinam, with its western border extending about ten miles from the Coppename River. In 1650, they founded the first permanent trading post in the north of the Suriname River, called Paramaribo, displacing the Dutch, who had been there intermittently since 1603. However, by the Treaty of Breda in 1667, Paramaribo was ceded to the Dutch by the British colonizer, Lord Willoughby, becoming the capital of Surinam. Before this, it had been an indigenous village, with the French briefly settling there in 1640. During the 18th and 19th centuries, the port of Paramaribo served as a hub for raw materials shipped by the West India Company. Fort Zeelandia was erected to protect against piracy, which was common due to European monarchs' encouragement of rivalries. Wars in Europe often spilled over into their far-flung colonies, leading to violence.

The West India Company encouraged planters and entrepreneurs from Europe to occupy land between the east bank of the Corentyne River and the lands granted to Lord Willoughby, ten miles from the west bank of the Coppename River. After 1667, Dutch governors in the region favored these settlers. Cotton, sugar, and dried fish, which were abundant, were shipped to Holland. Exotic woods, precious stones, minerals, and wild animals were also commercialized. As the Industrial Revolution in Europe gained momentum, trading in the Guianas became even more profitable. Planters sold their goods and raw materials to whoever was available.

Paramaribo, located just nine miles inland from the ocean, became an ideal storage and shipping center for raw materials produced by surrounding plantations. As the settlement grew, people of different nationalities were drawn to the area, finding employment in packaging, shipping, and cottage industries essential to the town's success. Paramaribo became a showcase for the West India Company in South America, boasting more economic activity and a larger population than any other place in Surinam, eventually becoming the capital city of Dutch Guiana.

During the First and Second World Wars, raw materials like cotton, wood, balata, and gold were in high demand in the Guianas. Dutch Guiana saw an influx of settlers; some came to make fast fortunes in the extractive industries, others to trade, and some to raise families and escape the horrors of the wars in Europe. Eventually, a government system was organized under the Dutch. They established post offices, police departments, financial ministries, universities, research centers, and hospitals. Roads were built from Paramaribo, linking New Nickerie, Apoera, Bromsbury, and other scenic interior destinations, which became tourist attractions. A botanical garden was established, meticulously collecting and recording plant species, creating one of the most detailed herbaria in the Guianas.

Before and after the Afobaka Dam was built to produce hydroelectric power, scientists from the University of Paramaribo studied the effects of large-scale flooding. The university also provided access to studies on controlling and eradicating bilharzia, a disease affecting South American rice farmers. It is spread by freshwater snails living in flooded rice fields and can penetrate human skin, causing neurological issues, joint pain, and, in some cases, gallbladder cancer and liver failure. The eastern bank of the Nickerie River was fertile with rice fields, and the rice mill at Wakamaing became one of the most successful in the Caribbean. Thousands of acres were cultivated, requiring crucial labor, which was brought from neighboring Berbice.

In the late 1920s, rumors of oil being found in the Guianas surfaced. Brazil, concerned about territorial integrity, initiated the demarcation of borders. Since the 17th century, ongoing wars between European powers had caused South American colonies to change ownership, leading to border disputes between British Guiana and Dutch Guiana—later the Republic of Guyana and Surinam. Attempts by colonial governors to establish definite borders, such as the 1899 meeting in New Amsterdam, Berbice, were void, as only European monarchs could rectify such matters. Thus, the Corentyne River region, before the Schomburgk Line, was considered "no man's land."

Land grants along the Corentyne River for sugar and cotton cultivation were leased to companies like Eliza E. Moary Plantations at 74 Village and Brooker at Skeldon Estate. Individuals who had completed their indentures also wished to own land, receiving parcels of Crown land from the British government. The fifty-mile stretch from Milfenna below Orealla to Skeldon was occupied by these grants.

The reservation at Orealla, which includes the village of Siparuta nine miles upstream, was set aside for the native peoples of Guyana. This reservation stretched from the Canje River in the west to White Hills near the Kabalebo River estuary in the south. British control over the Corentyne River was paramount. Miners, porkknockers, balata bleeders, timber grant owners, and wildlife traders all sought licenses from the British administrative office in New Amsterdam. Control and security of the Corentyne River were predominantly British Guyana responsibilities. The river and its hundreds of creeks, streams, and mini rivers within a 500-mile stretch, including the Curuni and Katuri Rivers, flowed directly into the Corentyne. However, on the eastern banks, there were a few Dutch outposts. At McLemmon, above the Three Sister Islands during colonial rule, a weather station operated, measuring rainfall within a 20-mile stretch.

The Amerindian reservations at Weshabo and Apoera had about fifty families who did not settle in one location permanently. They moved along the river, using resources where they were plentiful. Their slash-and-burn farming techniques prevented them from staying in one place, allowing them to move freely along the river without restriction from any administrative jurisdictions.

The use of the Corentyne River became a focus in the 1960s and 1970s when the Government considered relocating the capital of Paramaribo to Apoera. Streets were paved, electricity was supplied to each benab, modern hotels were erected, and the deepest and most modern wharf in the Caribbean was constructed. However, this project, into which millions of guilders were invested, ultimately failed.

In early 1936, a group of European leaders, including Dutch representatives, struggled to agree on the ownership of the Corentyne River. Their decision to allot the entire river to Surinam was met with British protests. The treaty was never ratified due to the outbreak of World War II. After the war, Holland was less inclined to oppose the British position on the Corentyne River, as they owed much of their survival to the English-led fight against Hitler's forces. In 1966, when Guyana gained independence, the Corentyne River was officially recognized as the eastern boundary of the new nation.

The boundary was marked at #61 on the west bank of the Corentyne River estuary, 10 degrees east of true north. In the years following 1966, the Dutch colony was allowed free use of the river, as there were no territorial disputes between the neighboring administrations. Suriname gained its independence in 1975, ten years after Guyana, and was expected to respect international norms regarding border recognition.

According to international custom, when two countries are separated by a body of water, the border is recognized at the deepest channel, or thalweg, between the shores. This practice continued until a few years after 1975, when Suriname, believing Guyana's internal parliamentary divisions weakened its resolve, began to assert claims over the entire river.

From 1966 onward, the Guyana Police Force enforced law on the river between Siparuta, Orealla, and Crabwood Creek. However, declining state funding for river patrols eventually led to weaker enforcement, relying on private crafts hired by the police force.

The Surinamese military presence in the Corentyne River increased in the 1980s, not to establish border integrity but to defend against the overthrow of the military government. During this period, illegal trade between Guyanese citizens and Surinamese businesses flourished, as Surinamese authorities protected the import of goods into Guyana. Fishermen, who traditionally sold their catch at #79 Foreshore, began taking part of it to Nickerie to earn guilders. They seized the opportunity to buy merchandise from local Surinamese stores, leading to wholesale cross-border trading.

Guyanese smugglers sold gold and diamonds to obtain Dutch guilders, which were then exchanged for Guyanese dollars at higher-than-bank rates. Surinamese businessmen sent guilders into Guyana, purchasing U.S. dollars from tourists and exports, further driving down foreign currency availability in Guyana.

In Suriname, the foreign currency acquired was used by businesses to import goods from Holland, such as potatoes, powdered milk, split peas, baking flour, and canned items. These goods were shipped to warehouses in Suriname and legally consigned to Guyanese businesses. Once in the custody of customs in New Nickerie, official request forms from Guyana were needed to release specified quantities. Daily, small boats crossed the Corentyne River, completing official procedures at immigration and customs to collect their goods, paying storage fees, and transporting cargo to various locations in Guyana. One customs official remarked, "More than a million U.S. dollars' worth of business is conducted daily," highlighting the economic impact on his town.

CHAPTER 3

The Corentyne River: A Borderline of Conflict and Commerce

In earlier years, New Nickerie was hardly known to most Guyanese. It was seen as little more than a two-street settlement, with a small waterfront landing zone for fishing boats, a police station, post office, a modest two-story administrative office, and one asphalt road capable of supporting heavy traffic. The few supermarkets in the area served the entire countryside west of Nickerie and carried only limited groceries and basic wares. However, the influx of Guyanese traders from Springlands on the west bank of the Corentyne River changed the town's dynamic, prompting a wave of new development.

A single motor launch made one trip across the 22-mile stretch of river each day, carrying double its safe capacity of passengers and baggage. As the flow of traders increased, businessmen in Suriname recognized the need for better accommodations. Hotels and inns were built to house overnight visitors and intermittent traders, while hardware stores, vehicle outlets, supermarkets, and fabric shops expanded to meet the growing demand. With Guyana experiencing severe shortages of basic goods, New Nickerie became a bustling trade center, with its shops filled daily with customers purchasing goods to take back across the river.

At the ferry staging area in Springlands, the tax office became a critical stop. Travelers required a tax clearance certificate to receive an exit stamp on their passports. The demand for these clearances led to long lines, with applicants sometimes queuing from midnight onward. Allegations of bribery at the tax office were rampant, with inspectors rumored to expedite clearances for those willing to pay. This led to widespread frustration among travelers and traders. "I've been waiting since 1 a.m., and it's nearly midday, and I still haven't seen the inspector," one traveler complained. Another replied, "If you bribe the inspector, you wouldn't be waiting." Many citizens expressed bitterness, vowing never to return to Guyana after enduring such ordeals.

The hardships of Guyanese traders fostered a growing sentiment of discontent. Many spoke openly about emigrating to Suriname, hoping for better opportunities. Some married Surinamese spouses, seeing this as a way to secure a brighter future for their children. The economic stagnation and social frustration in Guyana led to a gradual transformation in the population's social composition, with an increasing number of citizens seeking a better life across the river.

In Suriname, fishing was historically a small-scale, family-driven enterprise. However, the Japanese community introduced innovative techniques, honed by generations of experience. They used long wooden poles planted in mudflats to support funnel-like nets that captured fish and shrimp with the tidal flow. Villages with Japanese-Surinamese populations were easily identifiable by their distinctive architecture and the open platforms used for sun-drying shrimp. This delicacy, highly prized both locally and in Holland, was a major export product. Their narrow-hulled canoes, powered by small engines, allowed them to navigate shallow waters during low tide and operate in the swampy mudflats of Afdomen, catching tilapia, snook, and mullet.

Between Afdomen and Coronie Koker in western Suriname, a vast stretch of brackish swamp extended two miles inland from the ocean. The swamp fed into a river about 40 feet wide and 20 feet deep, navigable at high tide by crafts with drafts of up to 10 feet. Fishing on the coastal mudflats was perilous, with many paying the ultimate price. The ocean between the Orinoco River in Venezuela and French Guiana's western coast was rich in marine life but notoriously challenging. Silty waters deposited by the continent's rivers created fertile mudflats teeming with fish, sea turtles, and crabs.

Illegal fishing by foreign vessels was a longstanding issue. Factory ships from foreign nations sent trawlers into the region, dragging heavy nets across the seabed. These operations decimated fragile marine habitats, capturing and often killing juvenile fish, sharks, and sea turtles. This unsustainable practice significantly depleted fish populations, including blackfin sharks prized in certain cultures for their purported aphrodisiac properties.

By the late 1970s, Guyana's economic stagnation led to the mass migration of skilled labor. Farmers and fishermen abandoned the countryside, leading to shortages of animal protein. Local producers struggled due to a ban on imported livestock feed, making chicken, pork, cattle, and sheep both expensive and scarce. This situation pushed fishermen to focus on harvesting the ocean, where fish were abundant and affordable. Over time, fish became a staple protein source for Guyana's predominantly coastal population.

Small fishing vessels initially operated safely on the mudflats, but as demand grew, local craftsmen began designing sturdier boats capable of withstanding the Atlantic's harsh waves. These larger boats enabled fishermen to venture dozens of miles offshore, exploiting the rich fishing grounds on the continental shelf. However, the lack of government oversight and scientific guidance left the industry operating inefficiently and unsustainably.

In Suriname, the fishing industry lagged behind until the 1970s. Even by the early 21st century, few government officials understood the environmental damage caused by illegal foreign fishing operations. Meanwhile, Guyana's fisheries expanded, with enterprises like Corentyne Seafood adding prawn trawlers to their fleets and exporting to the Caribbean and the United States. Small fishing villages along the coast from Essequibo to Corentyne grew as private individuals invested in the lucrative industry.

Despite these developments, the fishing industry faced significant challenges. There was little training for ocean fishermen, no access to survival gear or radio communication, and no rescue system in place. Fishermen risked their lives for modest earnings, operating in dangerous conditions with no monitoring or support. This lack of oversight also allowed some fugitives to hide within the fishing community, further complicating the industry's challenges.

As Guyana and Suriname grappled with economic and environ-mental pressures, their fishing industries highlighted the delicate balance between opportunity and exploitation. Both nations faced the urgent need to implement sustainable practices, protect their marine resources, and ensure the safety of those who ventured into the unpredictable waters of the Atlantic.

CHAPTER 4

Blathole and the Rise of Fishing Piracy

In western Suriname, Guyanese fishermen found work with small-scale fishing operations. Many of them lacked legal status to work in the country but were willing to take the risks for an honest living. Their primary tasks involved venturing into the sea for dangerous fishing expeditions, a challenge they quickly adapted to. They spent weeks or even months at a time on shanty platforms over the water, immersed in the swamps of the Blathole. Over time, they mastered the geography and tricks of the trade, making the swamps their second home.

Fishing was not the only activity in these remote areas. Rumors circulated about contraband and smuggling operations, often involving men like Bald, a fisherman-turned-middleman, who was well-connected in the shadowy underworld. Bald frequently returned to his village to flaunt his earnings, recruit workers, and share tales of lucrative but risky ventures in Suriname. He claimed his employer, Marlon Pairam, was not just a wealthy fisherman but also involved in illegal arms trading, allegedly sourcing guns from Brazil and distributing them across Suriname.

Bald was a well-known figure in the fishing communities along the Corentyne. At 25 years old, he had already worked in over ten fishing locations, from Whim on the Corentyne to Anna Regina on the Essequibo Coast. He was regarded as a resourceful mechanic and problem-solver, often sourcing rare engine parts for fishing boats. However, his reputation extended beyond fishing; locals whispered about his connections to drug traffickers and smugglers operating across the Corentyne.

Marlon Pairam, a seasoned fisherman in his mid-40s, inherited his trade from his father and grandfather. He owned six platforms in Afdamen, each manned by two Guyanese fishermen. While his fishing operations appeared legitimate, Marlon was deeply entrenched in smuggling. Under the guise of fishing, his workers transported rum, sugar, and gold from Guyana across the Corentyne River. Hidden beneath dense mangrove canopies, these goods were ferried through the swamps to distribution points in Wakeman, Coronie, and Paramaribo.

Marlon's network operated smoothly for years until an incident in June 2001 exposed the risky nature of his enterprise. During the annual mullet migration, Doobay Singh and his crew decided to capitalize on the season. The mullets, feeding on the mudflats near "Bucks," attracted fishermen despite the area's dangerous reputation for quicksand and treacherous waves.

Doobay's crew, consisting of Jaffer, Sonny, Split Face, Long Head, and John Andrews, prepared for the trip with little hesitation. Over a bottle of rum in a makeshift bar, they discussed their plan. "This past month has been bad for fishing," Andrews remarked. "If we can catch mullet, we'll make enough to repair my motorbike." Encouraged, the crew loaded their boat, *Miss Mala*, with supplies, including a mile-long seine, poles, ice, and food.

The seine, a deadly fishing tool, was designed to trap anything caught in its circular path. Anchored in the mudflats, it funneled fish into a wide bag as the tide receded. Even small aquatic creatures caught in the net were killed, a testament to its efficiency—and brutality.

As the boat navigated the Corentyne River estuary, Andrews and Long Head alternated steering, while the rest of the crew organized the cabin and prepared for the night's work. Captain Doobay, an experienced fisherman, estimated they would reach the fishing grounds in about four hours. "Once we're there, I should be able to spot the shoals of mullet playing on the surface," he assured his crew.

Split Face, standing on the cabin deck, suddenly shouted, "Look! Qurimaan jumping!" A silver streak of mullet shot across the water, hitting Sonny squarely in the chest. The crew burst into laughter, teasing Sonny about his bad luck. "Don't worry," Captain Doobay said, "you'll have your revenge when we cook it for curry."

As night fell, the *Miss Mala* reached the fishing grounds. The crew anchored the boat half a mile from the shore and began setting the seine. Working quietly in the rain, they prepared the net's bottom cord, pinning it to the mud with hooked sticks. The upper cord was suspended by poles, creating a wide funnel to trap the fish.

The tide began to fall, and the crew worked methodically. Captain Doobay directed the operation while keeping a watchful eye on the horizon. "It's going to rain heavily," he warned, "but the ocean water is warm, so we'll be fine."

The rain arrived with thunder and lightning, but the crew pressed on. Long Head and Andrews worked tirelessly, washing and icing the catch, while the rest of the crew gathered fish from the seine. Despite the challenging conditions, the operation proceeded smoothly.

Fishing on the mudflats was not without danger. The powerful Atlantic waves and treacherous terrain posed constant threats. However, the promise of a good catch and the potential profits kept fishermen returning to these perilous waters. For men like Long Head and Andrews, who were new to the crew, this trip was a chance to prove their worth. Captain Doobay praised them as hardworking and reliable, noting their dedication to sending money back to their families in Mahaica.

As the crew waited for the next tide, they huddled in the cabin, joking and sharing stories to pass the time. The camaraderie among the men was evident, despite the hardships of their trade. For them, fishing was more than a job—it was a way of life, marked by risk, resilience, and the relentless pursuit of survival in the challenging waters of the Atlantic.

CHAPTER 5

A Haven for Buccaneers

The entrance to "Blathole" lies between two expansive natural mudflats. These stretch from the thin shell beach in the south, tapering flat to the water level in the north. In the center of this shallow mud valley is a channel, a natural drain carved by the runoff of swamp waters into the Blathole River. At low tide, this channel is barely noticeable, but at high tide, it becomes obscured by the rebounding crosswaves of the ocean. Only skilled seamen could navigate this perilous passage, threading their boats through the waves to access the river mouth. Once inside, the calm waters of the river offered secrecy that was nearly impenetrable.

The Blathole River is a concealed haven, hidden behind dense mangrove and courida canopies. Its channel stretches approximately 12 miles from east to west before emptying through a narrow, deep passage into the mudflats at low tide. From the sugar-brown western beaches of the Corentyne River estuary to the mudbanks at "Bucks," Blathole is nearly 30 nautical miles away. This remote location kept its existence known to only a few, mostly locals and those with criminal intent.

By the late 1970s and early 1990s, the growing congestion of fishing boats along the Guyana Shield coastline began to strain marine habitats.

Overfishing led to dwindling catches, creating financial hardships for fishermen. Small-scale fishing operations, desperate for manpower, started hiring anyone willing to work, opening the doors to criminal elements. The hidden swamps of Blathole became a fertile ground for illicit activities, providing refuge for pirates and smugglers who preyed on the struggling fishing community.

Criminal groups grew like a cancer among the fishing communities. Sponsored by shadowy backers, these pirates hijacked boats, stealing expensive machinery and reselling it whole or as spare parts. Their leaders grew wealthy, profiting from stolen loot and bloodshed. Some of these operations were linked to Blathole, where smugglers and pirates found safe haven.

Marlon Pairam stood out among these shadowy figures. His economic success was visible—he flaunted a luxury Tacoma truck, a green Mercedes-Benz, a Rolex watch, and even gold-plated teeth. Alongside his ostentatious lifestyle, he carried two semi-automatic pistols and an AK-47 with a modified magazine. His bodyguards, Rafael and Magro, were former cartel enforcers from Venezuela, sent by his newfound international contacts.

Despite his outward success, Marlon was under immense pressure. His secret hideout at Blathole, initially meant for a single operation, had become the center of recurring deals. One misstep in Venezuela had entangled him in debts worth millions of U.S. dollars. Now, his life was shadowed by the watchful eyes of his cartel-linked bodyguards.

Marlon's financial troubles deepened after the death of his parents. He inherited the family estate in New Nickerie, which he mortgaged for a loan of 200,000 guilders. The money was meant to develop rice fields and upgrade fishing equipment, but Marlon's compulsive gambling drained the funds within weeks. His friend, Sayid Sotok, a wealthy rice miller and secretive trafficker, lured him into a rigged card game. By the end of the night, Marlon had not only lost his bank loan but also owed Sayid an additional 50,000 guilders.

Sayid, however, had ulterior motives. His arms, drugs, and human trafficking operations needed a new hideout, and Marlon's control over the Afdamen swamps and access to the unpatrolled oceanfront made him an ideal partner. Sayid used the card game to bind Marlon into his web of criminal activity, offering him a lifeline when the debts became overwhelming.

Marlon trusted Sayid and saw his offer as an act of friendship. But as weeks turned into months and Sayid disappeared, Marlon realized the depth of his predicament. His business faltered, old machinery broke down, and workers left for better opportunities. The only asset he retained was the Blathole operation, a grim lifeline in an economy sinking deeper into stagnation.

Marlon relied heavily on a group of die-hard Guyanese fishermen who had worked with his father. These men, skilled in navigating the oceanfront from the Amazon to Venezuela, were invaluable. They knew every hidden creek and river and were unafraid to defend themselves. Old Pairam had warned Marlon about the crew's quirks before his death, advising him to treat them fairly but maintain control. "Their loyalty is unmatched," he said. "But they need clear plans to execute. If anything changes, they'll falter—or worse."

The crew's exploits became legendary. One tale involved Bruckup, a talented mechanic, who disregarded the plan during a raid. His actions woke a flock of guinea fowl, drawing gunfire from a frightened homeowner. Bruckup was shot in the thigh, but his crewmate Jaggie carried him back to safety. Old Pairam recounted the story as a cautionary tale: "Stick to the plan, or abandon it entirely."

The Corentyne fishing fleet had evolved over decades. By the 1980s, most boats were built with timber frames, measuring 80 feet long with sturdy greenheart keels and planks resistant to barnacle infestation. These boats were divided into sections for storage, sleeping quarters, and iceboxes. The iceboxes, designed to preserve fish for up to 15 days, were critical for maintaining the quality of the catch.

Fishing was a delicate balance of labor and capital. Owners provided boats, nets, fuel, and supplies, while captains and deckhands worked the ocean. Captains received a higher share of the profits for their leadership and responsibility. "The owner takes the biggest risks," Captain Larry explained during a trip. "If we lose a net or the boat is damaged, it's on him. Our job is to make sure we come back with a full load."

The fishing process was grueling. Nets, often three miles long, were cast into the water and left to drift for hours. Fish caught in the gill net were quickly gutted and iced to preserve quality. The crew worked tirelessly, enduring the harsh conditions of the open sea.

Despite the hardships, the camaraderie among the crew kept spirits high. During breaks, they shared stories and jokes, marveling at the beauty of the starlit sky. "The stars look like a trillion fireflies blinking at each other," Brusha mused one night, prompting laughter and banter from his crewmates.

Captain Larry, reminiscing about their early days, reflected on how much had changed. "We started with small boats and sails, fishing close to shore. Now we're out here with engines and iceboxes, catching enough to fill tons. But some things haven't changed—like the friendships we've built."

As the *Miss Nootoo* glided through the waves, the crew prepared for their next haul, bound by a shared determination to navigate both the challenges of the ocean and the complexities of their intertwined lives.

CHAPTER 6

Engineering Resilience

The large fishing fleet on the Corentyne primarily uses a standard size of fishing craft. Each boat is constructed with a wooden timber frame measuring sixty feet in length, with beams three inches thick and ten inches wide. The foundation of the craft is a sixty-foot-long greenheart keel, five inches high and three inches thick, prized for its strength and resistance to marine decay. A single mora stern plank, expertly crafted and bolted to the keel with a five-foot-long stainless steel custom-made bolt, ensures a smooth keel bottom, optimizing stability and performance.

Rising at the stern is a ten-by-ten-inch mora timber post standing twelve feet high. This is anchored securely to the forward top of the keel using four one-foot-long steel bolts, beveled into the greenheart keel for a watertight fit. A quarter-inch-thick felt layer is sandwiched between the stern base and the keel to enhance water resistance and seal the structure. Forty curved mora ribs form the boat's internal skeleton, providing a sturdy framework onto which the outer planks of the hull are meticulously nailed.

The outer planking, crafted from greenheart wood, extends up to the bridge turn, adding remarkable stability and durability to the vessel.

31

Greenheart's natural resistance to barnacles ensures the craft remains efficient and robust in harsh marine conditions. The construction also allows for slight flexibility, enabling the boat to absorb and withstand the impact of waves without compromising its integrity.

From the bilge turn up to the six-foot-high gunwale, the siding is made of lighter, more malleable boards. These are water-sealed using cotton strings lightly woven and hammered tightly into the seams. Once the craft is in water, the wood fibers swell, further tightening the seams and ensuring the hull remains watertight, even under the constant battering of the waves.

This intricate design, rooted in tradition and practicality, ensures the fishing boats of the Corentyne are not only functional but durable, capable of enduring the demanding conditions of the open sea.

The craft is divided into three main sections. The stern houses the cabin, which spans about a third of the boat's length and provides shelter and storage for the crew. Inside, temporary cross-boards double as bunks and storage spaces, offering a makeshift home during long fishing trips. The middle section of the boat is an open area where the seine—a three-mile-long fishing net—is meticulously packed and stored. Finally, the bow contains an insulated icebox where the catch is stored, preserving it for market.

Fishing operations are highly organized. When the seine is cast, it drifts with the ocean currents, trapping fish in its wide netting. The captain's expertise determines the net's depth and position, ensuring an optimal catch. The process requires teamwork: one crew member handles the "bottom cord," weighted to sink the net, while another oversees the "top cord," which keeps it afloat with buoys. After several hours of drifting, the net is hauled in, yielding the day's catch.

The division of labor is clear. The crew works in harmony to gut, clean, and ice the fish quickly to preserve quality. Each man knows his role, whether it's hauling in the net, processing the catch, or packing it in the icebox. As the work progresses, camaraderie lightens the burden of grueling hours.

"Brusha, you and Stoneface start picking up the seine," Captain Larry called out. "Rudy, clear the fish. Bigbelly, separate the guts. Davanand, pack the fish in the icebox."

Under Captain Larry's guidance, the crew functions like a well-oiled machine. His leadership is respected, not only for his ability to navigate the challenges of the open sea but also for his fairness. As per custom, the profits are shared equally after expenses, with the captain earning an additional 10% from each share for his responsibilities.

"Why does the captain get extra?" Davanand asked one day.

"Because he carries the greatest risk," Brusha explained. "Larry is responsible for the safety of the boat, the crew, and the catch. Without his experience, we wouldn't make it back with anything."

The camaraderie aboard the vessel is a source of pride for Captain Larry. Despite the hardships, he ensures every crew member feels valued. Nights on the boat often bring moments of reflection, with the men sharing stories under a canopy of stars, temporarily forgetting the grueling labor.

CHAPTER 7

Rudy's Legacy

The rhythmic lapping of the waves against the boat often created a sense of calm, but it was also a stark reminder of the unpredictability of the ocean. As the crew prepared for another day, Captain Larry turned to Rudy, his longtime friend and confidant.

"Rudy, how come you've stayed with us so long?" Larry asked, breaking the morning silence.

Rudy smiled, a mixture of nostalgia and melancholy crossing his face. "My grandparents came from Barbados to work on the sugar estates. I don't know much about my parents; they went into the interior to search for gold and never came back. Grandma used to say they'd show up one day with pockets full of riches, but that day never came."

He paused, gazing out at the horizon. "Grandpa and Grandma raised me, teaching me everything I know. We reared pigs and sheep, and for a long time, that was my life. But now, here I am with you lot, flying fish out of the sea."

The crew chuckled softly, sensing Rudy's attempt to lighten the mood. Bigbelly, always quick with a joke, piped up, "What did people do with pigs back then, Rudy? Use them as fishing bait?"

Rudy shot him a look of mock indignation. "Knucklehead, people eat pigs! Grandpa, bless his soul, once got so drunk on jamoon wine that he fell asleep on his cart while taking pigs to market. The donkey knew the way home better than him. Little boys played a prank and turned the cart back to the yard. When he woke up, he thought he'd reached the market and started hollering for customers to buy pigs. Grandma laughed so hard she nearly dropped the pot she was stirring."

The crew laughed heartily, the story bringing warmth to the cool morning. The camaraderie of the group was a salve for the hardships they faced, each man finding solace in shared humor and stories.

As the conversation shifted, Rudy's voice softened. "Millie, my eldest, is turning nine tomorrow. I wish I could be home for her birthday."

"You'll make it up to her," Stoneface reassured him. "What matters is that you're out here working to give her a better life."

Rudy nodded, though his heart ached with longing. "She's been having trouble with her eyesight. There's a specialist visiting at the end of the month. Between that and paying off the house, it's why I'm here, but sometimes I wonder if it's worth it."

"It is," Captain Larry interjected, his tone firm yet empathetic. "We all miss our families. But every fish we pull in, every trip we take, brings us closer to providing them with what they need."

The crew fell into a reflective silence, the only sounds the gentle splash of the waves and the occasional call of a seabird. These moments of introspection were rare but vital, reminding each man why he endured the ocean's hardships.

"Look alive, men," Larry said, breaking the stillness. "See those whitecaps ahead? That's the Bucks. One of the best fishing spots out here. Get ready to cast the seine."

The crew sprang into action, their earlier sentiments giving way to the focused energy of their labor. Brusha and Stoneface worked in tandem, casting the net into the rolling waves with practiced precision. The boat rocked violently, but the men moved with the rhythm of the sea, their muscles taut and their minds sharp.

As the net drifted with the current, the crew settled into a quieter pace, cooking a simple meal and chatting idly. The Bucks was both a blessing and a curse—a bountiful fishing ground but fraught with danger. The men were acutely aware of the stories, passed down from generations, of boats that never returned.

"Captain, how long have we been doing this together?" Bigbelly asked as they waited for the seine to fill.

"Feels like forever," Larry replied with a smile. "Back then, the boats were smaller, and we didn't even carry ice. We'd fish all day, sell what we caught, and start again the next morning."

The conversation turned to memories of their younger days, a time when the hardships felt less daunting and the rewards sweeter. As the sun dipped below the horizon, casting an amber glow over the water, the men were reminded of why they chose this life—a mix of adventure, necessity, and the unbreakable bond of brotherhood.

"Alright, boys," Larry called out, his voice carrying a note of optimism. "Let's reel it in and see what the goddess of the sea has given us today."

The crew moved as one, their camaraderie and shared purpose propelling them through the backbreaking labor. Each haul of the net brought the promise of a better tomorrow, even if it was laced with the salt of sweat and tears.

CHAPTER 8:

The Price of Survival

The calloused skin on their palms was as hard as the cowhide gloves they wore, or like discarded, dried-up turtle shells. Barehanded, the crew hauled in the bottom and top cords of the seine, starting from the end that was thrown overboard first. The moderately calm surface—with wave heights of about three or four feet—required three crew members to pull in half of the seine. Then, two fresh pullers relieved them, alternating to ease the strenuous labor of pulling the heavy boat across the waves.

The middle crew member stood inside the seine's bay, pulling the strock to sag the net and keep it level. Its belly, woven with twine, basketed the catch into the boat. The thick rope, weighted with leads and twine, pulled the catch from forty feet beneath the waves. The bulging seine worked the shoulders, arms, and backs of the crew like an athlete pulling a buggy cork fixed to the flooring. Hours passed as the laborious process of retrieving the seine continued.

The catch, once loosened from the net, was tossed into the adjacent "fish pen" under the bench, separated from the icebox. "Wow! You should be called strong arms and big shoulders!" Davanand commented to Bigbelly, admiring the rope-like, rippling muscles on his shoulders and biceps.

"Yes, man, but a false name is what it is—false," Bigbelly replied.

"What about me?" Davanand asked, curious to hear Bigbelly's wisdom.

"You're so ugly, and yet you get a starboy name," Captain Larry interjected jokingly over the quiet beat of the slow throttle of the outboard engine he was steering. Nearby, Stoneface and Rudy were gutting fish, separating swim bladders from the guts.

As the first fifty snapper, trout, and other catches were gutted and washed in seawater, the half-side covers of the icebox were opened. The cleaned fish were thrown into the ice. This process repeated several times, depending on the volume of the catch. By the end, when the seine was fully retrieved and all the fish cleaned, Captain Larry set a course and called on one of the crew to steer the boat. Bigbelly took the helm and guided them toward a red light, a blinking beacon high on a tower barely visible through dark, shifting clouds on the Surinam foreshore.

"I see it, Captain!" Bigbelly acknowledged, relieved to be free of the backbreaking pulling. "I'll help the boys ice down the fish while Davanand fixes something to snack on once we finish casting the seine again."

"We're going to cook," Captain Larry instructed, deliberately relieving the crew members who had been working strenuously. It was gestures like these that endeared him to the crew. "Captain, you're a fair person," Rudy said. "I love the way you divide the work. It makes everyone share the chores equally without feeling the pressure of working ten to sixteen hours a day."

The crew shouted their agreement. "That's the truth, Captain!"

Days turned into two weeks of grueling labor. A piece of the net was destroyed by sharks and needed mending, taking away time meant for rest after retrieving the net and saving the catch for market.

"Captain, we only have ice for about three more days, and the icebox is almost full of fish," Stoneface noted.

"I know you've missed your families, booze, fancy clothes, food, and the comfort of home. And, of course, the saloon floor," Captain Larry said, looking at Bigbelly when he mentioned the saloon. "But this is what we do. This is who we are. We've chosen to reap the bounties of the ocean, even at the cost of homely comforts. But think of the reception you'll get when you return home to your love!"

The crew nodded, comforted by Larry's words. "We'll be closer to the shores of Guyana soon. Just a couple of hours southward, and we'll be home."

Larry summarized their prospects. "We've got about five hundred marketable first-class snapper and a hundred pounds of swim bladder. We should get a good price for them."

"It's about three o'clock. We'll start picking up the seine around six, after the thunderclouds pass us," Stoneface predicted, shielding his eyes to look farther into the horizon. The clouds were heavy and black, touching the waves. "It will definitely rain," he concluded.

"You're right," Larry said, amused. "Because the earth is round, we can't see beyond the curve."

The eight-foot warp that tied the top end of the drifting net to the boat's stem held the craft like a kite anchored to a large string. It had to be long enough to allow the boat to crest and trough with the waves.

"Captain! I think I see a boat beyond the rain clouds," Stoneface said.

"Can you see the color of the flag or the boat?" Captain Larry asked as the other crew members continued their chores.

"No, Captain," Stoneface replied. "There's no flag."

"This is the ocean, boys! Boats don't have license plates," Davanand said, vindicating his wisdom.

"The boat might be looking for a seine that's cut loose," Rudy reassured.

"Whoever it is will know we're here from the markings on our floats," Captain Larry assured the crew. He stretched out flat on the aluminum decking, relieved after hours of tedious labor.

The rain began to fall, heading directly for them. Sheets of raindrops blurred visibility and drowned out all sound. Everyone dove into the cabin as thunderous clouds shook their eardrums. Lightning bolts seared the air, leaving the smell of nitrous oxide in their wake. The cabin filled with the deafening sound of rain pelting the galvanized roof. Wind gusts whipped the waves into a frenzy, sending the boat pitching up and down in eighteen to twenty-foot swells. Inside the cabin, pots and pans clattered, and the crew clung to the inner railings to keep from being tossed around.

As the storm calmed slightly, the rhythmic drumming of rain on the roof created a soothing melody. The crew huddled in the cabin, passing around pastries and cream soda. "At least it will be warm tonight if the rain stops," Davanand remarked, munching on a piece of pastry.

Suddenly, Captain Larry's ears perked up. "I can hear the beat of an outboard engine," he said.

The rain poured relentlessly, soaking Captain Larry's head and shoulders as he braved the storm. The sharp crack of an AK-47 bullet tore through the air, breaking the sound barrier and briefly overpowering the rumble of thunder and lightning. Larry lost his footing as the boat's bow plunged into a deep wave trough, sending him tumbling into the water. For a fleeting moment, he caught sight of a dark, shadowy craft amidst the chaos, its shouts muffled by the storm.

Explosive volleys of gunfire shattered the night, jolting the crew into frantic action. Rudy instinctively poked his head out of the cabin to check on Larry. A single 10mm bullet struck him, ripping through his neck with devastating force. The impact severed his windpipe and obliterated his C3 and C4 vertebrae, leaving a gaping hole and rendering him lifeless. Blood sprayed like a ruptured hose, painting the cabin walls as Rudy's body crumpled backward. The grotesque gurgling of his last breaths, choked by clotted blood, produced an eerie, terrifying sound that froze the remaining crew in their tracks.

Inside the cabin, the four remaining crew members screamed uncontrollably, their wails rising above the thunderclaps. Gunfire continued to echo, amplifying their terror. Masked Man #1 leapt from the shadowy craft onto the top of the icebox, brandishing a double-barrel shotgun. "Shut up! Shut up!" he barked, his voice slicing through the chaos. He aimed the shotgun menacingly at the cowering men. "Come out with your hands up!"

Masked Man #2 skillfully maneuvered the smaller craft alongside the fishing boat, keeping it steady despite the chopping waves and relentless rain. Masked Man #3 jumped onto the fishing boat's cabin roof, tying the two boats together with a sturdy line. At the same time, Masked Man #4 leapt cat-like into the empty seine pen. Finally, Masked Man #5 climbed aboard, his imposing figure armed with a two-bladed machete. The pirates moved with practiced precision, each carrying two pistols holstered on green canvas belts and wearing life jackets strapped tightly to their chests.

Stoneface, trembling with fear, crawled out of the cabin. Masked Man #3 slammed the flat side of his machete against Stoneface's back, then grabbed his hair and tossed his nearly paralyzed body into the empty seine pen. Stoneface shrieked in agony as he hit the wooden floor. Moments later, Davanand, Bigbelly, and Brusha followed, each receiving the same brutal treatment. They lay motionless, paralyzed by pain and terror.

"Now, girls, get up and stop squealing like boneless worms!" Masked Man #3 sneered, taking command of the pirates. He pointed at Bigbelly and Brusha. "You two, get over to our boat and remove the engines. Pass them across, or I'll take your heads off!" To emphasize his point, he fired a round from his AK-47 into the fishing boat's side, creating a hole that allowed seawater to trickle in. "Move, your miserable pieces of refuse!" he shouted.

Bigbelly and Brusha scrambled to obey, jumping onto the pirate craft. They began loosening the heavy 48- and 75-horsepower Yamaha outboard engines. The boats bumped and swayed violently in the rolling waves, making the job treacherous. The unsteady movement caused the men to fall repeatedly, each time narrowly avoiding being crushed by the machinery. The pirates lashed their machetes against the fishermen's backs, urging them to work faster. "Move, you motherf***ers! Work like you have life!" one of the pirates roared.

After transferring the first two engines, the pirates ordered the crew to remove four additional engines stored in the cabin. The relentless waves and heavy rain made the task even more dangerous, but the crew worked as quickly as their trembling hands would allow. Masked Man #1 surveyed the pirate boat, shouting, "All of you, get back over here!" He fired another round into the air to enforce obedience.

Once the crew was back on the fishing boat, the pirates ordered them to lie flat on the floor. Using machetes, the pirates cut pieces of coiled rope and quickly tied the fishermen's hands and feet. The bindings were pulled tight, cutting into their skin. "Please, sir, don't hurt me anymore! I have small children to care for!" Brusha pleaded, tears streaming down his face. "In the name of God, have mercy!" Bigbelly added, his voice trembling.

"We're poor men trying to make an honest living," Davanand begged. "This boat doesn't even belong to us. Please, just give us one life jacket. We won't tell anyone what happened!"

The pirates ignored their cries. Masked Man #1 snarled at his crew, "How long are you going to listen to these miserable bitches? Finish tying their feet!" The fishermen's screams grew louder as the pirates looped the ropes tighter, binding their hands and feet together behind their backs like animals prepared for slaughter.

The rain intensified, hammering against the cabin deck. Masked Man #4 retrieved four heavy sandbags from the pirate boat's stern and tied a twenty-foot rope to each one. He passed the ropes to the other pirates, who worked quickly, fastening them to the fishermen's bindings. The fishermen sobbed and wailed, their cries blending with the thunder and the relentless drumming of the rain. "Oh God, please help me!" Davanand cried, his voice breaking.

The pirates gave each other a thumbs-up, satisfied with their grim preparations. The fishermen's bodies were tossed and slammed against the cabin floor as the waves rocked the boat. Lightning flashed across the dark horizon, illuminating the horror unfolding on the deck. For a brief moment, the storm seemed to hold its breath as the pirates dragged the sandbags to the edge of the boat. One by one, they heaved the bags overboard. The ropes snapped taut, yanking the bound fishermen off the deck and into the churning ocean. Their screams were silenced as the sandbags dragged them beneath the waves.

"Cut the bowline and stern line!" Masked Man #1 commanded. The pirates severed the ropes connecting the boats. The fishing vessel, now riddled with bullet holes and rapidly taking on water, began to sink. The pirates fired a few more rounds into their hull before starting their engine. "You've done a good job," Masked Man #1 said as they sped away, disappearing into the dense swamp of Blathole, leaving nothing but the storm and the sinking boat behind.

CHAPTER 9

The Storm, the Shadows, and the Promise of Home

Captain Larry's sharp ears picked up the humming beat of an approaching outboard engine. Too close for comfort. A warning instinct flared in his mind. Something about it felt wrong. In the thick darkness, with rain sheeting down in torrents, visibility was already low. The seine was still tied to the boat, its long wrap stretching out beneath the waves. If the oncoming craft tangled its propellers in the line, there would be no choice but to cut the net free. The loss would be devastating.

In this stormy weather, the risk was even greater. An engine fouled by rope could spell disaster—a boat disabled, vulnerable to capsizing in the high waves, leaving its crew stranded or drowned. If they lost the seine, there was no telling when they'd find it again. Drifting in open waters, three miles of net could disappear beneath the vast expanse of the ocean, never to be recovered. Searching for it would be like looking for a grain of sand in a bag of rice.

And yet, that wasn't the worst of it. This was their last pickup of the trip. Their gasoline was nearly finished. The ice box was packed with fish, meant for the morning market sale. If something went wrong now, they wouldn't just lose their equipment; they'd lose their entire haul—days of work, their only means of income.

Larry inhaled deeply, steadying himself. His thoughts flickered to Celia. He had twenty-seven years of experience as a sea captain, had spent much of his life braving the waters of the Caribbean and the Atlantic, but it had been *her*—his Celia—who had changed his course entirely.

He could still remember the moment they met, a memory so vivid it cut through the present storm like a warm sunrise.

It had been a rainy afternoon, just like this one. He had been half-soaked, sprinting across the street to escape the downpour, not noticing the delicate figure in front of him until—*bam!* He crashed straight into her, nearly knocking her over. His reflexes kicked in, catching her just in time before she fell.

"Oh! I am so sorry!" His words tumbled out in an embarrassed mumble, his brain scrambling to form a coherent apology.

She looked up at him, dark hair dripping, eyes shining with curiosity and amusement, and in that moment, Larry forgot the rain, forgot the world, forgot how to breathe.

"Yes, you were," she replied, a playful lilt in her voice.

Larry, usually composed, found himself stammering like a boy. "I—I didn't see you. I wasn't looking. I—"

"Clearly," she teased, tilting her head.

He had knocked her umbrella from her grasp, and now she stood there, soaked, blinking at him. Flustered, Larry bent quickly to retrieve it, handing it back with an apologetic smile. *"Here. And—here, take this too."* He pulled a dry white cotton handkerchief from his pocket.

Her fingers brushed his as she took it. "Thank you."

"I'm Larry," he blurted. "A friend of the rain god."

Her brow lifted. "A friend of *who*?"

He grinned. "I prayed for the most beautiful, ravishing, breathtaking woman in the world to cross my path today. And here you are."

She laughed, shaking her head at his boldness. "You sure know how to flatter a girl."

"It's not flattery. It's truth," he said, his Eastern European accent giving his words a dreamlike charm.

That was the moment Celia Beck became his entire world.

He had followed her directions to the market street, where she lived in a modest two-story home above her family's shop. Their courtship was brief but intense. Celia was unlike anyone he had ever met—sharp-witted, fiercely independent, yet soft in a way that made him feel safe. She loved the sea almost as much as he did, though she feared its dangers.

He could still picture the evening he proposed.

51

They had been sitting on the Springlands Stelling, watching the muddy spring tide crash against the wooden pillars below. Celia had been leaning over the railing, the wind teasing her hair. She was waiting for him—waiting too long. *Why do men do that?* she had thought, *don't they know how embarrassing it is for a girl to stand alone on the stelling?*

She had just started to blink back tears when his fingers brushed against her ear. The moment she spun around, she threw her arms around his neck and began to cry.

"Come now, my love bug," he had murmured, kissing her damp cheeks, his arms wrapping around her small frame. *"I was just hiding behind that post, watching you, trying to make myself small."*

She playfully hit his arm but held on tighter.

Larry had gotten down on one knee, his heart pounding. *"Celia Beck, will you marry me? I will love you and care for you, only you, for all the days of my life."*

Her gasp turned into laughter, and before he could even process what was happening, she leaped into his arms, nearly knocking them both over.

"YES!" she cried.

Applause erupted from the onlookers at the Stelling. Celia had been beloved in the community, and now they were all witnesses to their joy.

Their simple wedding had been held at the village Catholic church, with Celia's family and a few of Larry's relatives from Roraima in attendance.

That had been the happiest day of his life.

And now—here he was, clinging to a sinking net in a raging storm, possibly about to die.

The thought hit him like a bullet to the chest. *Celia. The boys. I can't leave them.*

He forced himself back to the present, scanning the darkness. The pirates, because that's what they were on his boat now, transferring equipment and fish into their own craft. He could hear the screams of his men, pleading for their lives.

Then the unmistakable crack of gunfire.

Larry's entire body seized in horror.

One by one, his crew was silenced.

His breath came in short gasps. His hands trembled against the cold wet rope of the net. If they saw him—if they found him in the water, it would be over.

His only chance was to move.

Beneath the rain and gunfire, he slipped into the ocean, silent as a ghost.

The water was warm, warmer than the icy fear curling in his gut.

He swam toward the floating buoy at the end of the seine, knowing it was his only lifeline. He had to survive. He had to get back to Celia. To his sons.

Not tonight. Not like this.

With one final burst of strength, he reached the buoy, clutching onto it as if holding onto life itself.

In the distance, the pirates' boat disappeared into the night, leaving behind nothing but bodies, a sinking vessel, and the rolling storm.

Larry was the only one left alive.

And as the rain poured down, as the ocean rocked him like a child in a cradle, his mind clung to one thought only. *Celia. I'm coming home.*

Chapter 10

Captain Larry's Journey

Larry clung to the buoy as the waves heaved and rolled, their rhythm both comforting and disorienting. The storm had finally begun to dissipate, and the first faint glow of dawn painted the eastern horizon. The ocean, though still turbulent, was slowly calming. Exhaustion pulled at every fiber of his being, but his mind remained sharp, haunted by the events of the previous night.

The crew's voices still echoed in his ears—their cries for mercy, their anguish as they were bound and sent to their watery graves. The sight of the pirates' boat speeding away played on an endless loop in his mind. Larry's fingers dug into the buoy's rope as anger and grief warred within him. He resolved, once more, that he would survive—for them and for the family waiting for him onshore.

As the light grew stronger, Larry began to take stock of his situation. The buoy had drifted miles from the wreckage. He couldn't see the boat, the seine, or any sign of the pirates. It was just him, the open ocean, and the floating marker tethered to the remnants of his net below.

He knew he couldn't stay on the buoy forever. The currents could carry him farther out to sea, into deeper and more dangerous waters. His best hope was to steer toward the distant coast, where he might find help, or at least a chance of survival.

With effort, Larry began to paddle, using his legs to push the buoy in the direction he hoped was west. The motion was slow, agonizing, but it gave him purpose. The sun climbed higher, its heat beating down on his saltwater-soaked skin. He welcomed its warmth, though it drained his energy further.

Hours passed. Larry's strength was fading, and his mind wandered. He thought of Celia and the boys; her smile the way she held their sons close at bedtime, her soft voice urging him to be careful every time he left for sea. The thought of never seeing them again twisted his heart. He clenched his jaw and forced himself to keep going.

The distant hum of an engine startled him. He froze, his ears straining to locate the sound. It grew louder and closer. Larry's pulse quickened, was it another pirate boat? Or, by some miracle, was it a friendly vessel?

He waved an arm, the effort nearly draining the last of his energy. The sound of the engine grew louder still, and soon, a small fishing boat appeared on the horizon. Larry felt a surge of hope.

The boat's crew spotted him and quickly maneuvered to his side. Two men leaned over, pulling him aboard. Larry collapsed onto the deck, too weak to speak. The fishermen gave him water and wrapped him in a blanket. One of them, an older man with weathered hands and kind eyes, knelt beside him.

"You're lucky we found you," the man said, his voice gruff but warm. "What happened out there?"

Larry could only manage a hoarse whisper. "Pirates... they took everything."

The men exchanged grim looks. "We've heard of these attacks. You're not the first. They've been preying on boats all along the coast."

Larry's hands balled into fists. "My crew... they're gone. They killed them all."

The older man placed a steadying hand on his shoulder. "We'll get you to shore. You'll need to tell the authorities."

As the boat approached the coastline, the sight of land brought tears to Larry's eyes. He had survived the impossible, but the weight of his loss pressed heavily on him. The fishermen helped him ashore, and he was soon taken to the local authorities, where he recounted the harrowing events in as much detail as he could manage.

But even as he spoke, Larry knew that justice would be hard to come by. The ocean was vast, and the pirates were skilled at disappearing into its shadows. Still, he vowed to do whatever it took to protect others from suffering the same fate.

That evening, as the sun dipped below the horizon, Larry returned home. Celia met him at the door, her face a mixture of relief and disbelief. She threw her arms around him, holding him as though she'd never let go. The boys clung to his legs, their tears soaking his clothes.

"You're safe," Celia whispered, her voice breaking. "You're home."

Larry held them close, his body trembling with emotion. He had made it back, but he knew the scars of that night would stay with him forever. He had faced the darkness of the ocean and the cruelty of man and though he had survived, he would never forget the cost.

CHAPTER 11

The Emerald Network: Treachery Among the Canopies

The horizon began brightening in the eastern sky, the rising sun casting a breathtaking spectrum of colors across the sea. The clouds reflected hues like a living rainbow, but the beauty of the morning was overshadowed by a sense of mortal fear. Larry clung tightly to the flagpole, his body pressed against its base, wishing he could disappear. He feared the pirates would see him, and every passing cloud's shadow felt like a spotlight exposing his vulnerability. Immersing himself in the water was not an option; letting go of the floating base meant certain death by drowning.

The sun rose steadily, illuminating the horizon, but ominous black clouds rolled in from the north. Larry prayed fervently for rain. "Dear God, Jesus, please let it rain," he whispered, his voice trembling. Rain, he knew, would conceal him from any prying eyes. His only chance of survival was to stay afloat and hope to reach land by God's grace.

His eyes burned from saltwater spray, stinging as the relentless waves tossed him up and down. By midday, the sun's harsh glare reflected off the water's surface, creating a blinding, mirror-like effect. Larry squinted against the light; his vision reduced to the short distance of each cresting wave. Years of experience working these waters told him land couldn't be far, yet he was acutely aware of the dangers: sharks lurking below and the pirates who might investigate the fluttering yellow flag above him.

Suddenly, the heavens answered his prayers. Sheets of heavy rain poured down, obscuring the horizon in a white haze. The fresh water cooled his parched skin and washed away the dried salt that had clung to him. The rain offered both relief and hope, momentarily masking his fear of exposure.

The wind calmed, and the rain thickened. Larry noticed the waves growing shallower, perhaps an indication that he was nearing land. But fear clawed at his mind: "Think of your family," he urged himself. "You must survive for Celia and the children. You have to tell the world what happened to your friends." His thoughts turned to God. "Lord Jesus, if you save me, I will dedicate my life to good deeds. Please save me."

As if in answer to his pleas, a flash of lightning illuminated the horizon, followed by a deafening crack of thunder. Then, a sudden, cold brush against his leg sent a chill through his body. Larry curled into a fetal position, gripping the flagpole like it was his lifeline. The shadow passed beneath him again, and he screamed, his mind racing with images of shark attacks he had seen before.

But the threat turned out to be something miraculous: dolphins. A playful pod of them surfaced around him, nudging the styrofoam base as if curious about its strange occupant. Larry's fear transformed into desperate gratitude. "Stay with me! Don't leave me, my beautiful, beautiful friends," he cried.

But his relief was short-lived. A distant disturbance in the water caught his eye, a massive tiger shark breached, snatching a baby dolphin in a flash of ferocity. The water turned red, the blood spreading like a sinister stain across the waves. Larry froze in terror, clutching the flagpole as if it could shield him from the predator's deadly reach. Memories of shark attacks flooded his mind: men losing limbs, boats overturned. His prayers grew more desperate. "Dear God, I don't hate them—please spare me from this!"

As night fell, the rain subsided, revealing a glittering canopy of stars above. Larry took solace in their beauty, though their brilliance only deepened his sense of isolation. The southern cross twinkled faintly, a familiar guide, but he felt the cruel irony of its distant light. He thought of the countless nights he had admired the stars from the safety of his boat and wished he could return to those peaceful moments.

Hours passed, and Larry drifted into a swift current. The floating base spun slightly, signaling that he might have entered the mouth of a river. Dawn broke, revealing the faint lights of prawn trawlers on the horizon. Larry recognized these vessels—massive floating factories that stripped the ocean bare with their nets. He had heard harrowing stories of these operations, how they worked relentlessly, processing every creature caught in their nets, from fish to endangered turtles.

Larry's hope and dread warred within him. If the trawlers saw him, they might rescue him or they might kill him to silence any witness to their illegal activities. His heart raced as he clung to the flagpole, praying that God would hide him from their view.

The trawlers' lights grew dimmer as they moved further north. The day wore on, and the relentless glare of the sun returned. Larry closed his eyes, his body battered and exhausted. He whispered one final prayer, "Lord, if I survive this, I will never take life for granted again."

CHAPTER 12

Winds of Change in the North Akari

Celia paced her small room, tears streaming down her face. She avoided her children, unwilling to scare them, as they happily planned an outing with their father to visit the local farms. But her heart was heavy with worry. Larry was four days overdue.

The owner of Larry's boat, Mr. Thakar, had visited the day before, his concern poorly masked. "I'm sorry to worry you, Mrs. Larry," he said, shifting uncomfortably. "It's just that, at sea, even small things can go wrong. But your husband is an experienced captain."

In truth, Mr. Thakar was deeply worried. Two other boats from the fleet had been missing for over two weeks. Efforts to locate them through messages sent to Paramaribo, the Essequibo, and even Trinidad had yielded nothing. He didn't want to alarm Larry's family further, but the situation was dire. "Larry's boat may have gone to the capital of Surinam to sell their catch and restock ice before heading home," he speculated aloud, trying to reassure himself as much as Celia. "This has happened before, and communication from Paramaribo to Guyana is notoriously unreliable."

Celia asked quietly, "Are you sure Larry decided to do a double trip?" Her voice trembled. "He wasn't feeling well before he left. I

63

begged him to stay home, but he wouldn't listen. He said the children needed school supplies."

"The arrangement was for a single trip," Thakar admitted, "but sometimes captains make that call at sea. It happens." He hesitated, then added, "We're organizing a search. Several boats will be sent out to look for them in case of engine trouble or drifting with the tide."

Under Mr. Thakar's stilted reassurances, Celia detected his underlying fear. He addressed the crew's families who had gathered under his stilted house, their faces etched with anxiety. Across the fishing community, the number of missing boats had grown to six.

On the open sea, Larry's body had grown stiff. His salt-encrusted fingers were fused to the metal flagpole he clung to for survival. His eyelids, crusted with dried salt, remained shut to protect his eyes from the relentless glare of the sun. Rain finally fell that night, in a merciful downpour that washed the salt from his skin and allowed him to open his eyes.

When he regained some semblance of awareness, he felt something different beneath him. His body was no longer bobbing with the waves. Was it possible he had reached land? Slowly, he stretched out a trembling hand. It met something firm. Sand. Wet mud. Could it be true? He sat up, clutching the flagpole for reassurance, as distant flickering lights caught his eye.

The lights moved—sometimes swiftly, sometimes slowly. It had to be people! Gathering his strength, Larry began dragging himself toward the lights. Each step was agony. The mud sucked at his legs like quicksand, threatening to trap him with every step. But the flagpole provided balance, its heavy base preventing him from sinking completely. "Don't stop," he told himself. "Think of Celia. Think of the children."

Reaching the edge of a fast-moving stream, Larry plunged forward, using the flagpole to stabilize himself. He crossed, his weak body trembling, and stumbled onto firmer ground. Ahead, the lights grew brighter. As he neared the source, he shouted hoarsely, "Help! Please help me!"

"Who's there?" a voice called back.

"Water," Larry croaked, his throat too dry to say more.

The figures drew closer, their flaming torches illuminating the night. "It's Larry!" one of them exclaimed. "My cousin Rudy works with him!" The crab catchers sprang into action. One washed the mud from Larry's face while another handed him a water bag. Slowly, Larry took a sip, his parched throat savoring the liquid relief.

"This man is from the #43 fisheries," one of the crabbers said urgently. "We've got to get him to the Port Mourant Hospital. He's in bad shape." They helped Larry walk the half mile to the hospital, where doctors immediately began treating his severe dehydration and exhaustion.

News of Larry's ordeal spread quickly, making headlines across the region. For weeks, the police showed interest in his account, but the investigation soon fizzled. The other members of his crew were undocumented and known only by aliases. The incident occurred in international waters, leaving little jurisdiction for authorities. Without witnesses or evidence, Larry's story was considered unverifiable. The families of the missing crew members were too impoverished to push for answers, and the region's naval patrol was minimal at best.

In the aftermath, Larry and Mr. Thakar made the difficult decision to leave Guyana. They migrated to another country, carrying with them the memories of a harrowing ordeal and the unanswered questions that haunted them.

CHAPTER 13

Children of the Shadows

The men were asleep, sprawled across the deck, their steady breathing blending with the rhythmic lapping of the waves. Captain Doobay sat alone on the cabin roof, savoring the cool Atlantic breeze. Above him, the stars sparkled like scattered diamonds, their brilliance unmarred by city lights. To the north, the faint green and yellow lights of trawlers glimmered on the horizon, scraping the seabed for its marine treasures. Beyond them, the glow of offshore oil rigs illuminated the night sky, signaling the encroachment of industrial progress.

Doobay's thoughts turned to the street-radio chatter he'd overheard about Guyana's potential oil wealth. "They say we're floating on oil," he murmured to himself, a wry smile tugging at his lips. "Richer than Venezuela, they claim." But his amusement was tinged with sadness. He'd read the warnings: drilling miles beneath the ocean floor was a perilous endeavor, and a single mistake could unleash an environmental catastrophe, polluting the Caribbean Sea for decades. Even without oil spills, the invasive grasses and contaminated ballast water from tankers posed a grave threat to the fragile ecosystem.

Why, he wondered, would anyone gamble the region's fertile fishing grounds for a fleeting windfall of oil money? Thousands of livelihoods depended on the sea, yet decisions about its future seemed to be made far away, by people who would never feel the loss. Glancing at his sleeping crew, he felt a pang of helplessness. The destruction of their environment felt inevitable, a tide too powerful to resist.

A measuring pole caught his eye, jolting him back to reality. The boat had grounded, and it was time to work. "Alright, girls!" he called down to the crew with mock cheerfulness. "Time to wake up. The tide's gone, and we're stuck until we haul in the catch!"

The men stirred, groaning and stretching before slipping into the slick mudflats. Jafro and Splitface took the right side of the seine net, while Longhead and Andrews worked the left. The warm mud squelched beneath their feet, clinging to their skin like a sticky second layer. The net was alive with trapped mullet, their frantic thrashing echoing across the flats.

"Every five minutes," Doobay said, tipping a twenty-pound box of mullet onto the ice, "and we'll have a good haul before the sun ruins the catch." By daylight, their work grew easier without the need for torchlight, but the sun's heat threatened to spoil the fish left too long in the net. The crew moved quickly, knowing they'd lose much of the catch despite their efforts.

"We're destroying more than we can take," Longhead lamented, handing a bucket of croakers and mackerel to the captain.

Doobay nodded solemnly. "This type of fishing is wasteful, but it's what we can afford. Until someone in authority stops it, we're stuck with it."

The crew fell into a resigned silence, their movements efficient but joyless. The tide had receded completely, leaving vast expanses of mudflat exposed to the merciless sun. "It's like a mirage on the road," Andrews observed, sweat glistening on his forehead, "only this one's on the mud."

"The Atlantic breeze is gone, too," Splitface muttered. "It's like the sea is punishing us for the carnage we leave behind."

Doobay glanced at his men with a heavy heart. "We're poor men trying to survive. We do what we must, but it doesn't mean we like it."

Their conversation was interrupted by Splitface pointing eastward. "Captain, look! Are those people walking on the mud?"

Doobay shaded his eyes and chuckled. "No, those are flamingos. They're common here along the northern Amazon. Their long legs make them look like people from a distance."

Jafro chimed in, eager to share his knowledge. "Once, we caught one in the net. Its legs got tangled, and we cooked it. Bony, but it tasted alright."

From a hidden perch in the mangroves, a pair of eyes watched the fishermen's every move. Mr. Montane muttered to himself, "This isn't good," before hurrying back to camp. There, he relayed what he'd seen to Ruda, who immediately sounded the alarm. "Van's crew needs to know," Ruda said, urgency sharpening his tone. "Call them now."

When Van picked up the phone, Ruda's voice was uncharacteristically forceful. "We need to meet immediately. This is serious."

"I'm busy," Van protested. "Why can't it wait?"

"No excuses," Ruda snapped. "Hemar Bridge. One hour. Be there."

Van sighed, sensing the tension in Ruda's voice. "Fine. I'll come," he conceded, though he loathed being dragged from his plans. He knew Ruda wasn't one to overreact, and the growing pressure within their network left no room for error.

As Van prepared to leave, he couldn't shake the nagging fear that this meeting might involve more than a simple update. With stakes as high as they were, any misstep could have deadly consequences.

CHAPTER 14

Whispers of the Black Hole Swamp

Kurt Shalim was the sole surviving member of his family. The memories of his childhood were seared with tragedy. He was only twelve years old when his father and two older brothers were killed. According to the Portuguese owner of the Akari Mines, Hans Boet, it was a tragic accident. The limestone tunnels had collapsed, their walls unsupported by timber reinforcements. Everyone who worked the rugged, diamond-rich concessions of Brazil knew the dangers. Caves-ins were frequent, and life was cheap in this part of the world.

The Portuguese brought brutal labor enforcers, armed with superior firepower, to oversee the mines. These guards were ruthless, ensuring that no resistance would interfere with operations. They were the first foreigners brought to the Akari jungle, stationed at a makeshift camp near the Rio Pueblo riverbed. A rusted zinc sheet sign at the camp's entrance advertised the need for skilled miners, promising good pay and humane working conditions.

Kurt's father, desperate to provide for his family, signed himself and his three underage sons up to work for Boet's mining company. The hiring clerk assured him the boys would be paid the same rate as adults.

Their duties would be light—errands mostly—but the promise of steady income for his family was too tempting to pass up.

"My company will be the wealthiest in South America," Hans Boet had boasted. "Diamonds, gold, and emeralds, all of it waits in the Akari Mountains." But Boet conveniently omitted the grueling conditions under which these treasures were extracted. The workers faced sweltering heat, swarms of disease-carrying mosquitoes, and the ever-present threats of dysentery, yellow fever, and malaria. The jungle was a living hell, where every step could bring danger.

Two months before Kurt and his family arrived, Boet sent in a pioneering work crew. This twenty-man team, led by a renegade Panamanian Carib named Itus, was tasked with setting up operations deep in the jungle. Itus had years of experience navigating the Akari wilderness, though his history was checkered. He had acted as a guide on a failed diamond expedition years earlier and had a reputation for being as cunning as the predators of the jungle.

Hans Boet had learned of the Akari Mountains' treasures from traders who spoke of the legendary caves guarded by the mysterious Arapas tribe. "The walls glitter like rainbows in the evening sunlight," one trader had said, handing Boet a frosted stone as proof. The chief of the Arapas had drunkenly boasted about the gemstones, claiming the caves were filled with jewels and gold. It was enough to ignite Boet's greed.

The journey to the Akari jungle was an odyssey in itself. Boet's hired crew traveled by helicopter, their equipment and supplies flown in from the town of Itica, five hundred miles south of Boa Vista. The trip to the mining site required traversing leech-infested swamps, quicksand, and dense undergrowth. Itus, acting as their guide, warned them of the dangers: venomous plants, massive anacondas, and jaguars prowling the dense foliage.

Of the original twenty-six members of the expedition, including ten native guides, only eleven reached the grassy knoll at the base of the Katuri Cataracts. Eight men had been lost to quicksand, natural traps of venomous leaves, and snake bites. One man, overcome by the hopelessness of their trek, had taken his own life.

By the time they reached the first ridge of the Akari Mountains, the group was battered and demoralized. The terrain grew increasingly treacherous as they climbed. The dense canopy overhead blocked out the sun, creating an eerie twilight even at midday. The air was thick with humidity, and every step required hacking through a web of vines and bamboo.

Itus recounted the horrors of the journey with a detached tone, but his eyes betrayed the trauma he had endured. "The natives we brought with us were treated cruelly," he admitted. "They carried the heaviest burdens, were cursed and spat upon. Even their women were taken by the foreigners in full view of their partners." His voice faltered momentarily. "I was no better," he confessed. "I regret what I did, but regret does not undo the past."

By the time they set up camp on the first ridge, the natives had had enough. Under the cover of darkness, they fled, taking vital supplies with them, including food, cooking utensils, and medication. Their absence was discovered the next morning, leaving the remaining members of the expedition ill-prepared for the trials ahead.

The group pressed on, their numbers dwindling with each passing day. The jungle claimed them one by one—some fell to illness, others to accidents. By the time they reached the Katuri Gorge, they were down to a handful of weary survivors. Crossing the gorge was a daunting task, requiring them to climb ropes across the sheer cliffs while battling malaria and exhaustion.

Itus described the moment they first saw the glimmering entrance of the caves. "It was as if the mountain itself was alive," he said. "The walls shimmered with light, the colors dancing like fireflies in the dark. But the beauty was a cruel illusion."

Inside the caves, they found what they had come for, diamonds embedded in the walls like constellations frozen in stone. Yet the riches came at a price. The air was damp and stifling, and the floor was slick with water. Itus recalled how the group, desperate for rest, had lit a fire near the entrance, only to be forced out by rising water from a sudden rainstorm. They left the caves in disarray, losing valuable equipment in their rush to escape.

The horrors of the expedition haunted Itus long after he returned. "We left the jungle with fewer than half of the men we started with," he said. "And those who made it back were shadows of their former selves—broken, scarred, and haunted by what we had seen."

As Kurt listened to Itus recount the tale years later, he understood the weight of his father's decision to bring his family into such a world. The Akari Mountains were both a promise and a curse, their riches guarded by the unrelenting forces of nature.

CHAPTER 15

The Fire That Burned Truth to Ashes

The men began to show signs of fatigue, their morale weakened by the relentless hardships of the jungle. The few natives who remained carried the heaviest burdens—both physical and emotional. They moved with downcast eyes, their spirits crushed by the abuse from the foreigners. The humiliation of watching their women forced into submission in full view of the group only deepened their despair.

Itus, reflecting on those days, spoke with a mix of guilt and detachment. "I was part of their suffering," he admitted. "I don't deny it. I regret it now, but regret changes nothing."

The expedition's progress was slow. The dense undergrowth and towering trees formed an impenetrable wall, forcing them to hack a narrow path with machetes. Each step was a battle against the terrain, and every man was consumed by the gnawing fear of what lay ahead. When night fell, darkness swallowed the forest entirely. The thick canopy blocked out even the faintest starlight, leaving the camp in an oppressive gloom.

Their makeshift shelters offered little protection from the elements. Rain fell in torrents, soaking their gear and extinguishing their fire. The jungle came alive with eerie sounds, the calls of unseen birds, the chirping of insects, and the distant growls of predators prowling the night. The men huddled together in silence, each man lost in his thoughts, wondering if they would see another sunrise.

One night, the natives slipped away. Their departure was silent but deliberate, leaving the rest of the group to fend for themselves. It wasn't until morning that the absence of their guides and supplies became apparent. The remaining men, now reduced to a handful, were left vulnerable and exposed.

"We should have posted guards," Itus admitted bitterly. "It was a basic rule of survival we ignored. Exhaustion made fools of us."

The loss of the natives was a turning point. Without their knowledge of the land, the expedition's survival seemed doubtful. Yet, the group pressed on, driven by desperation and the allure of the treasure they sought.

The Akari Mountains loomed ahead, their peaks shrouded in mist. The journey to the ridge brought new challenges. The granite formations were sharp and unforgiving, the cliffs treacherously steep. Crossing the Katuri Gorge required scaling the ropes they had brought, but not all made it across.

"It was as if the mountain itself was testing us," Itus said. "Every step forward came at a price."

By now, malaria had taken hold of the group. The men suffered from fevers and chills, their bodies weakened by the relentless march. Itus, however, had remembered an old remedy taught to him by his elders. He found bark from the guanine tree, which he brewed into a bitter tea to ward off the disease. It wasn't a cure, but it kept him alive.

The group reached the summit of the ridge, where they gazed down into the valley below. The Katuri Cataracts roared in the distance, their thunderous waters carving a path through the jungle. For a moment, the men felt a glimmer of hope. The sight was breathtaking, a reminder of the beauty that existed even in the harshest of places.

But the jungle's dangers were never far. As they descended, the group encountered fresh challenges. One man fell victim to a nest of marabunta ants, his screams echoing through the trees as the swarm devoured him alive. Another succumbed to the poison of a venomous plant he had unwittingly touched. The jungle spared no one.

The men who survived the descent reached a clearing by the gorge. Here, they found traces of the Arapas—footprints in the sand and signs of a recent camp. Itus recognized the marks immediately.

"These people are legends," he told his companions. "They're said to be one with the jungle. If we cross their path, we must tread carefully."

The group moved cautiously, wary of being seen. But it wasn't long before they were surrounded. The Arapas emerged from the undergrowth, their spears tipped with sharpened bamboo, their faces painted with streaks of ash and dye. The foreigners had no time to react before they were bound with vines and led into captivity.

The Arapas held the group in a small cave, its entrance sealed with a spiked bamboo gate. The air inside was damp and stifling. The men huddled together; their fear palpable. Itus, however, saw an opportunity.

"I spoke to them in their tongue," he recounted. "My mother was of their people. Her blood runs through me."

The revelation startled the Arapas, who were not expecting to find one of their own among the captives. Itus pleaded with them, spinning a tale that painted the foreigners as lost traders who had come in peace. His words bought the group time, but he knew their survival depended on the goodwill of the Arapas' shaman.

The next day, Itus was brought before the shaman, a commanding figure adorned with necklaces of yellow gold and frosted stones. The shaman's eyes were sharp, his demeanor both intimidating and curious. Itus bowed low and began to weave a story that would determine the fate of his group.

"We come to trade, great one," he said. "We seek friendship and protection. We have no desire to harm your people or your land."

The shaman listened in silence; his expression unreadable. Then, he spoke. "We shall see if your words are true."

CHAPTER 16

Echoes in the Wilderness

The accommodations of the Arapas were extraordinarily simple, almost primal in their design. There were no structured huts or thatched roofs like those found in other Amazonian villages. Instead, rudimentary lean-tos, made of sapling poles and tightly stacked palm fronds, provided basic shelter against the elements. The fronds formed walls against the wind and rain, their greenish-brown hues blending seamlessly into the surrounding jungle.

Inside a cavern near the settlement, the shaman held court. His presence was commanding, almost mystical. His long, braided dreadlocks coiled around his neck like a ceremonial scarf, and a necklace of yellow gold nuggets rested against his broad chest. His waist was wrapped in a cloth of woven fibers, and his piercing eyes betrayed both wisdom and power. He radiated authority, making Itus feel small and exposed in his presence.

"What is your purpose here?" the shaman asked, his voice deep and measured.

Before his captors could speak, Itus stepped forward, bowing low. "Great one, we come as friends," he began, speaking in the broken dialect of the Arapas. "We are lost travelers, sent by our people to seek trade and protection. We mean no harm."

The shaman regarded Itus carefully, his expression inscrutable. "You speak well for an outsider," he said. "But words are easy. We will see if your actions match."

The Arapas allowed the captives to stay but kept them under constant watch. The foreigners were fed roasted wild game, tropical fruits, and nuts gathered from the surrounding jungle. Itus marveled at the efficiency of the tribe, who seemed to live in perfect harmony with their environment. Their diet was rich and diverse, sustained by their deep knowledge of the land's resources.

The shaman took particular interest in Itus, recognizing something familiar in him. "You are not like the others," he said one evening. "Your blood carries the mark of our people."

Itus nodded, seizing the opportunity to earn the shaman's trust. "My mother was of your tribe," he said. "She taught me your ways, your language. I carry her spirit with me."

The shaman's stern expression softened slightly. "If this is true, you may prove useful. But your companions…" He paused, his tone growing sharp again. "Their intentions are suspect. What do they seek in our mountains?"

Itus hesitated, knowing the wrong answer could seal their fate. "They are fools," he said finally. "They believe the stones and metals of this land hold power. But I know the truth—they are mere decorations, nothing more."

The shaman laughed, a deep, resonant sound that echoed through the cave. "You speak wisely, young one. These foreigners worship things they do not understand. But they will learn."

As days passed, the Arapas began preparing for their seasonal migration. The shaman explained that the big rains were approaching, and the lowlands would soon flood. The tribe planned to move east to the Mugot Mountains, where they would feast on the eggs of nesting turtles along the sandy shores.

"The mountains hold what your companions seek," the shaman told Itus one evening. "The caves are full of the yellow metal and colored stones they desire. But to us, they are mere playthings for children and adornments for our women."

Itus listened intently, filing away every word. The shaman described the tribe's trading history with foreigners who had come centuries earlier, exchanging tools, salt, and vibrant cloth for the precious stones. "They went mad for these things," the shaman said, shaking his head. "We gave them what we had, but their greed was endless."

The shaman's tone grew grave. "Be warned, young one. Those who covet the earth's treasures often meet a tragic end. Greed blinds them to the dangers that lie beneath the surface."

When the rains began, the Arapas led the captives to the caves, their movements purposeful and swift. Itus noted the tribe's meticulous organization. Each member carried their share of supplies—dried food, tools, and weapons—ensuring their survival during the migration. The captives were instructed to carry their own burdens, a gesture that both humiliated and humbled them.

The caves were exactly as the shaman had described. Their walls glittered with veins of gold and embedded gemstones, their colors shimmering in the faint torchlight. The foreigners were awestruck, their greed ignited. But the Arapas showed no interest in the treasures. To them, the caves were shelters, sanctuaries from the rains.

The shaman allowed the captives to gather a small portion of the stones as a gesture of goodwill. "Take what you can carry," he said. "But remember my warning: greed will destroy you."

The rains intensified, turning the jungle into a maze of swollen rivers and flooded paths. The Arapas navigated the terrain with ease, their canoes gliding through narrow waterways. The captives, however, struggled to keep up. Itus stayed close to the shaman, earning his favor with displays of deference and gratitude.

One night, as the rain poured in sheets, the shaman pulled Itus aside. "You have earned my respect," he said. "But your companions are not welcome here. Their greed will bring ruin to this land."

"What will you do with them?" Itus asked cautiously.

The shaman's eyes darkened. "That is not for you to decide. You are free to leave, but your loyalty to these men will determine your fate."

Itus nodded, understanding the weight of the choice before him. As he lay awake that night, he thought of the shaman's warning and the lives already lost on their treacherous journey. The jungle, he realized, had no mercy for those who took more than they needed.

CHAPTER 17

The Caves of Akari: Tunnels of Tragedy

The shaman's voice echoed through the cave as he summoned the captives for a fateful council. Itus and his companions were led into the heart of the mountain, where flickering flames illuminated the towering stalagmites and glinting mineral veins. The atmosphere was tense, the air thick with moisture and apprehension.

The shaman addressed Itus directly. "You claimed these men are here to trade and seek friendship. Yet their eyes betray their intentions. They covet what does not belong to them." He gestured toward the glittering walls. "Do they think the mountains will simply surrender their treasures?"

Itus bowed his head, choosing his words carefully. "Great one, they are blinded by the myths of their people. They believe these stones hold power, but they do not understand the dangers of the jungle."

The shaman's gaze softened slightly. "You speak with wisdom, child of the Arapas. But your companions are another matter. Their presence here cannot be ignored."

The shaman turned to the council of elders, who sat cross-legged in a semicircle. They whispered among themselves in a language foreign even to Itus. Finally, the shaman raised his hand, silencing the murmurs.

"We will give them a chance to prove their intentions," he declared. "If they seek the stones, they must journey to the northern cataracts. There, they will find what they desire—or meet the fate they deserve."

The captives were allowed to prepare for the journey. The Arapas provided basic supplies—water, dried meat, and bamboo spears—but warned them of the dangers ahead. Itus was torn. His allegiance to the foreigners was tenuous, but he understood the jungle better than they did. Without him, they had little chance of survival.

"You do not have to go with them," the shaman told him. "You are free to stay with us."

Itus hesitated. The offer was tempting, but he knew the consequences of abandoning the group. If they failed to return, the blame would fall on him. "I will guide them," he said finally. "But I will also honor your wisdom, great one."

The shaman nodded, his expression unreadable. "May the jungle show mercy on you all."

The journey to the northern cataracts was grueling. The jungle seemed to conspire against them, throwing every obstacle in their path. The heavy rains turned the ground to thick mud, and the swollen rivers became treacherous to cross. The group moved slowly, their progress hampered by exhaustion and fear.

As they descended into a narrow gorge, the air grew cooler, and the sound of rushing water grew louder. The cataracts came into view, their powerful currents carving deep into the rock. The scene was both breathtaking and ominous.

"This is it," Itus said, gesturing to the towering falls. "Beyond this point lies the territory of the wild."

The foreigners looked at each other nervously. They were out of their depth, and they knew it. But greed drove them forward. They began searching the rocky banks for signs of the gemstones they sought, oblivious to the dangers around them.

Itus watched them from a distance, his instincts on high alert. The jungle was alive with movement—birds scattering, leaves rustling. Something was watching them. He felt it in his bones.

Suddenly, a sharp cry pierced the air. One of the men had slipped on the wet rocks and tumbled into the rushing water. The current swept him away in an instant, his screams swallowed by the roar of the falls.

The remaining foreigners froze, their faces pale with terror. Itus stepped forward, his voice steady but firm. "You have to stop this," he said. "The jungle does not forgive. If you continue, you will not survive."

But his words fell on deaf ears. The men, desperate and driven by fear, continued their search. It wasn't long before another cry rang out. This time, it was an attack. A swarm of marabunta ants descended on the group, their stings sending the men into a frenzy. Itus yelled for them to stay still, but panic overtook reason.

Two men ran blindly into the undergrowth, their screams fading as the jungle claimed them. Itus turned to the remaining two, his voice rising. "Stay with me! Do not move unless I tell you!"

By the time night fell, only three remained—Itus and two foreigners. They huddled in a small clearing, their bodies trembling from exhaustion and fear. Itus kept watch, his ears attuned to the jungle's nocturnal symphony.

In the distance, the faint glow of bioluminescent fungi dotted the forest floor, casting an eerie light. Itus thought of the shaman's warning. The jungle was merciless, and they were intruders in its domain. He wondered if this was the fate the shaman had foreseen.

At dawn, the group pressed on, their path leading them deeper into the gorge. The air grew heavy, and the scent of decay lingered. They stumbled upon a clearing littered with bones—remnants of animals and, disturbingly, humans.

"This is a warning," Itus said grimly. "We are not welcome here."

The foreigners, now too frightened to protest, followed his lead. They moved cautiously, their eyes darting at every sound. The jungle seemed to close in around them, its dense foliage pressing like a shroud.

When they reached the northern ridge, Itus stopped. Before them lay a series of caves, their entrances partially hidden by thick vines. The walls glittered faintly in the dim light, hinting at the treasures within.

"This is what you came for," Itus said, his tone heavy with resignation. "But I warn you—nothing in this jungle comes without a price."

The foreigners hesitated, their greed warring with their fear. Finally, one stepped forward, his hands trembling as he pushed aside the vines. The jungle watched silently as the men entered the cave, unaware of what awaited them within.

CHAPTER 18

The Cost of Innocence

The rains intensified as the group descended deeper into the jungle. Torrents of water carved new paths through the land, transforming dry trails into rivers and low-lying areas into swamps. Itus and the remaining two foreigners trudged forward, their bodies battered by the relentless downpour and their minds weighed down by fear. Every sound, every shadow, seemed a threat in the ever-darkening jungle.

The northern ridge loomed ahead, its jagged silhouette partially obscured by mist and rain. The caves, Itus knew, were near. He also knew the jungle was watching, waiting for the trespassers to make one wrong move.

"We're almost there," Itus said, his voice low but firm. "But remember—the dangers inside the caves are as great as those we've faced out here."

The foreigners nodded, their faces pale and drawn. They had long since abandoned their bravado, replaced now by a grim determination to survive. The greed that had driven them into this wilderness had turned into a quiet desperation.

When they reached the caves, Itus stopped at the entrance, motioning for the others to stay back. He peered inside, his keen eyes scanning the dark recesses for signs of movement. The air inside was cool and damp, carrying the faint metallic tang of minerals.

"These caves are sacred," he said, turning to the others. "The Arapas see them as places of power and protection. If you disrespect them, the jungle will respond."

The men exchanged nervous glances but said nothing. One of them stepped forward, drawn by the faint glitter of gold veins running through the rock walls. He reached out tentatively, his fingers brushing the cold surface.

Itus sighed. "Take only what you can carry. Anything more will be your undoing."

The men worked quickly, chiseling small nuggets of gold and prying loose gemstones embedded in the walls. The caves glimmered faintly in the torchlight, the minerals reflecting a kaleidoscope of colors that seemed almost otherworldly. But the beauty of the place was deceptive. The deeper they ventured, the more oppressive the air became.

Itus stayed near the entrance, his instincts urging caution. He had no desire to linger in this place. The jungle outside had grown eerily quiet, its usual cacophony of sounds replaced by an unsettling stillness.

As the men gathered their haul, a faint tremor rippled through the ground. Itus felt it first, his body tensing as the vibrations grew stronger. "We need to leave," he said sharply. "Now."

The men hesitated, their greed outweighing their sense of danger. "Just a little more," one of them said, his voice trembling. "We came all this way…"

Itus stepped forward, his voice rising. "The mountain is warning us! Do you want to die here?"

Reluctantly, the men gathered their tools and began making their way back toward the entrance. But as they did, the tremors intensified. Rocks began to fall from the ceiling, and the faint trickle of water turned into a steady stream, pooling rapidly at their feet.

"Run!" Itus shouted.

The group scrambled out of the cave just as a section of the ceiling collapsed behind them, sending a plume of dust and debris into the air. The rain outside had grown heavier, and the ground beneath their feet was slippery and unstable.

"We can't stay here," Itus said, his voice urgent. "The mountain is collapsing. We have to move."

The foreigners followed him, their steps unsteady as they navigated the treacherous terrain. The jungle seemed alive with movement, the shadows shifting and twisting as the storm raged on. Itus felt the weight of the jungle's judgment bearing down on them.

They reached a small clearing, where Itus stopped to catch his breath. The rain had eased slightly, but the tension in the air remained. He turned to the men, his expression grim. "This is your last chance," he said. "Leave the stones behind. They are not worth your lives."

One of the men hesitated, his hands clutching a small pouch filled with gold and gemstones. He looked at Itus, then at the pouch, and finally at his companion. "He's right," he said, dropping the pouch onto the ground. "It's not worth it."

The other man shook his head. "We didn't come all this way to leave empty-handed." He tightened his grip on his own pouch and took a step back, distancing himself from the others.

Itus watched him carefully. "The jungle takes what it wants," he said softly. "It always does."

They continued their journey, the tension between the group palpable. The man who refused to leave his pouch grew increasingly paranoid, his eyes darting at every sound. Itus noticed his movements becoming erratic, his breathing shallow and quick.

By the time they reached the riverbank, the man's paranoia had turned into outright panic. He clutched his pouch tightly, muttering to himself as he scanned the surrounding jungle. Itus tried to calm him, but it was no use.

Without warning, the man bolted into the undergrowth, his movements frantic. "Wait!" Itus shouted, but the man was already gone, swallowed by the jungle's dense foliage.

The remaining man looked at Itus, his face pale with fear. "What happens now?" he asked.

Itus shook his head. "We move forward. The jungle will decide his fate."

They built a makeshift raft from bamboo and vines, using the river's current to carry them downstream. The journey was perilous, the waters swollen and fast-moving. But Itus's knowledge of the jungle guided them safely through the rapids.

When they finally reached a quiet stretch of river, the remaining foreigner turned to Itus. "You saved my life," he said, his voice filled with gratitude. "I won't forget this."

Itus nodded but said nothing. His thoughts were on the jungle, the shaman's warnings, and the lives that had been lost. He knew the jungle had claimed its price, as it always did.

As the river carried them toward the edge of the jungle, Itus felt a strange sense of relief. The mountains, the caves, and the shadows of the Akari were behind them now. But the lessons of the jungle would stay with him forever.

CHAPTER 19

The Bond of Blood and Betrayal

The river widened as Itus and the remaining foreigner drifted downstream. The jungle's density began to thin, its towering trees replaced by shorter, scrubbier growth. The rain had subsided, leaving behind a mist that clung to the water's surface, lending the scene an ethereal quality. Itus steered the bamboo raft with practiced ease, his sharp eyes scanning the banks for signs of danger or safe passage.

The foreigner sat hunched at the back of the raft, his expression a mixture of exhaustion and disbelief. The journey had stripped him of his greed, replacing it with a somber gratitude for his survival. "How did you know?" he finally asked, his voice breaking the long silence.

"Know what?" Itus replied without looking back.

"That the jungle would take its toll. That we wouldn't leave unscathed."

Itus paused, his hands tightening on the pole he used to guide the raft. "The jungle speaks if you're willing to listen. It has rules, like any other place. Those who ignore them… rarely make it out alive."

The foreigner nodded, his gaze fixed on the water. "The others didn't understand."

"They didn't want to," Itus said bluntly. "They came for gold and jewels, not wisdom."

By mid-afternoon, the river had carried them to a wide expanse where the current slowed. In the distance, the unmistakable signs of civilization came into view—a collection of huts perched on stilts, smoke curling lazily from their chimneys. The sight filled the foreigner with hope, but Itus remained wary.

"Stay close," he warned. "Not all settlements welcome outsiders."

As they approached, a group of fishermen spotted the raft and called out in a language unfamiliar to the foreigner but recognizable to Itus. The fishermen gestured for them to dock, their curiosity piqued by the sight of the weary travelers.

Itus secured the raft and stepped onto the muddy bank, addressing the fishermen in their native tongue. "We come in peace," he said, spreading his hands in a gesture of openness. "We are travelers from the north, seeking rest and passage."

The fishermen eyed them skeptically but eventually nodded. One of them, an older man with a weathered face, stepped forward. "You may stay," he said. "But do not bring trouble here. We've had enough of it."

The settlement was modest, a small cluster of homes built on raised platforms to withstand the seasonal floods. The villagers eyed the newcomers with suspicion but offered them food and water. Itus ate sparingly, his thoughts preoccupied with the journey ahead.

The foreigner, however, devoured the meal hungrily, his gratitude evident. "This feels like a dream," he said, looking around at the simple yet vibrant life of the village. "After everything we've been through…"

"It's not over yet," Itus interrupted. "The jungle may be behind us, but its reach is long. We need to stay vigilant."

That evening, as the villagers gathered around a fire to share stories, Itus approached the elder. "Have you seen others pass through here recently?" he asked.

The elder shook his head. "Not for many seasons. Why do you ask?"

"There were more of us when we began," Itus replied. "They didn't make it."

The elder studied him carefully. "You've seen the Akari, haven't you?"

Itus nodded. "We passed through the northern caves."

The elder's expression darkened. "That land is cursed. Those who go there rarely return. You are lucky to be alive."

"Luck had little to do with it," Itus said. "We had to earn our way out."

The elder sighed, his weathered features softening. "The jungle tests everyone who enters it. Some it spares. Others it claims. It's always been that way."

The following morning, Itus and the foreigner prepared to leave. The villagers provided them with a small canoe and directions to the nearest trading post, where they could arrange for passage back to civilization.

Before they departed, the elder pulled Itus aside. "You carry the jungle with you," he said. "It will guide you, but it will also haunt you. Remember that."

Itus inclined his head in acknowledgment. "Thank you."

As the canoe pushed off from the shore, the foreigner turned to Itus. "Will you go back?"

"To the jungle?" Itus asked, his tone flat. "No. It's taken enough from me."

The journey downstream was uneventful, the calm waters a stark contrast to the chaos they had left behind. By the time they reached the trading post, both men were physically and emotionally drained. The foreigner, grateful for his survival, promised Itus a share of the gemstones he had managed to save. But Itus refused.

"I didn't do this for payment," he said. "The jungle gave me enough."

"What will you do now?" the foreigner asked.

Itus looked toward the horizon, where the dense green canopy of the jungle faded into open plains. "I'll find my way," he said. "Like I always have."

CHAPTER 20

The Journey of Samara 2

Hans Boea's operations were meticulously organized. He dealt directly with recruiting, training, and conditioning young talent to fill positions within his illicit workforce. Liquidating rogue partners and associates was a routine part of maintaining his network. After losing his family, Kurt Shalim became a destitute orphan, a situation that Hans exploited. He saw potential in young Kurt, molding him through training and education into a loyal asset for his operations.

Hans harbored no tender feelings; his greed left no room for familial attachment. His female contacts were treated as property, conditioned to obey his every command. He viewed the young girls under his control as merchandise to be sold to the highest bidder. Virgins, unspoiled by experience, were particularly valuable—worth more than the gemstones Hans had acquired from Itus. These "merchandise" were part of a broader trafficking network that ensured Hans' wealth grew exponentially.

Itus played a pivotal role in Hans' operations. He had proposed using abandoned caves in the Akari region as training and conditioning camps. Hans found the idea ingenious. Hidden from aerial surveillance, the caves became a hub for operations ranging from human trafficking to storing contraband gemstones. The caves had previously been mined for their natural resources but now served as a secret base for Hans' expanding empire.

The MV *Samara 2*, one of Hans' key vessels, was loaded with $500 million worth of raw gemstones and life cargo. The vessel followed a carefully mapped route through the dense Amazonian waterways, relying on the cover of night to avoid detection. Its previous trips had been flawless, delivering both gemstones and trafficked individuals to prearranged locations. However, the increasing demand for Hans' "merchandise" put immense pressure on his network, requiring precision in recruitment, training, and shipment.

Years earlier, a break-in at the government offices of citizenship registration had resulted in stolen blank passports and birth certificates. Before an investigation could begin, the office was mysteriously set on fire. This and similar incidents created a perfect cover for Hans' activities, enabling him to forge identities for his trafficked individuals.

Despite their success, the network faced challenges. Economic hardship, rampant corruption, and environmental destruction in the region fueled Hans' supply chain. Greedy politicians and the disillusionment of the populace created a surplus of vulnerable individuals—ideal for exploitation.

Hans operated with caution, insulating himself from his illegal activities. Publicly, he was a benefactor of environmental causes, even gaining accolades for his support of wildlife preservation. Privately, his clandestine operations in North Akari flourished, bolstered by bribery, blackmail, and coercion. Itus and Kurt Shalim, Hans' trusted operatives, ensured the smooth functioning of this empire.

The caves, hidden deep within the jungle, became a fortress of horrors. The "life cargo," carefully selected and conditioned, were shipped from these hidden strongholds. The girls, subjected to brainwashing and abuse, were prepared for the final leg of their journey to international buyers. Hans' empire thrived on the ruthlessness of its operatives and the secrecy of its operations.

CHAPTER 21

The Hands That Feed the Shadows

The group of children wandering the market stalls were a pitiful sight—dirty, dressed in rags, and hungry. They played hide-and-seek among the backs of vendors and shoppers, their day a competition to see who could beg the most. Their wide, appealing eyes and outstretched hands often tugged at the hearts of strangers. Yet, behind this pitiful scene lay an insidious control. The children belonged to no one but the streets, sleeping in abandoned buildings or wherever they could find shelter from the elements. The lack of care exposed them to disease, malnutrition, and predators in a society whose officials were too preoccupied with personal gain to intervene.

Mala, an eight-year-old girl, had only faint memories of a caregiver she called Old Chonti. She and five other abandoned children, all cared for by the elderly woman, formed a fragile family. Old Chonti had found Mala as a baby, left in a cardboard box outside a mandir. She recalled nursing the baby on fruit juice until someone donated milk from a nearby hospital. "You screamed like your lungs would burst," Old Chonti often told her. "I had no choice but to keep you."

The small group survived on emotional bonds and their collective determination to make it through each day. But survival meant they often resorted to begging, their little earnings feeding the family and keeping them afloat. Yet as the children grew, their youthful innocence became a curse—they were becoming targets for predators.

One night, as the children huddled together under a makeshift shelter, Old Chonti and the other nannies had an ominous conversation.

"Those people who took Nanie and Garuda last year came back," Old Chonti began. "They made a good offer for Mala, Kamlish, and Tena. They say they will give the children a better life in French Guiana. The others they took before—they've all become rich and married to good families."

The nannies added their voices, recounting how the others had never returned. Some sent money, but it was clear they had moved on and forgotten the hardships of their past. "We have no choice," Old Chonti said tearfully. "This life is too hard. Let's hope they have a better chance out there."

The children listened in silence, their small hearts heavy with fear. Mala, the oldest, promised herself she would one day come back for Old Chonti and the others. The next night, as midnight approached, a car arrived to take them away. The children were blindfolded and warned to stay silent.

The journey was terrifying. They were loaded onto a small boat and told that any sound would lead to their deaths. Mala begged for her life, only to be shoved into a corner with a sharp reprimand. As the boat moved through the dark waters, whispers on a two-way radio made her ears perk up. A chilling command was issued: "Get rid of one." Moments later, the splash of a little boy's body into the water confirmed her worst fears.

When they reached the shore, the children were carried through the swamp to avoid alerting anyone nearby. They were transferred to a hidden camp where they were fed and allowed to sleep. Mala noticed the absence of Ratesh, one of her companions. She dared not ask questions, fearful of punishment.

Soon, they were blindfolded and loaded onto a helicopter. The ride was bumpy and disorienting, but eventually, they landed at a concealed cave. The children were stripped of their identities and given new names. Two harsh matrons barked orders, punctuating lessons with brutal whippings. "Yes, ma'am! No, ma'am!" became the children's mantra, their minds broken by fear and pain.

The conditioning was relentless. They were taught strict obedience, and mistakes were met with merciless punishment. Over the years, the children matured into their teenage forms, their physical beauty overshadowed by the emotional void left by their harrowing experiences. As they reached the final stages of conditioning, they became valuable "products" ready for sale. Those deemed unfit for market were discarded, often as entertainment for their captors or eliminated entirely.

Mala, though physically transformed into a graceful and striking young woman, had become hollow inside. She moved mechanically, her spirit long since extinguished. For her and others like her, the cave was not just a prison—it was a relentless machine that stripped away humanity to create commodities for the highest bidder.

CHAPTER 22

Itus: The Snake in the Canopies

The power over life and death is the ultimate authority, and for Itus, this power was not born from love but from control. He remembered hearing a Djuka elder once say, "The creator's power is love," and though he dismissed it as primitive morality, the words lingered. Itus wielded his power with cruelty, inflicting torture and pain, not for necessity but for the pleasure it brought to his twisted mind. He was a tool in Hans Boea's grand design, an instrument of meticulous precision and ruthless efficiency.

The caves, hidden deep in the Akari mountains, were an essential component of this sinister operation. Discovered years ago by Itus, these caves were not natural—they bore signs of ancient craftsmanship. Hans Boea recognized their potential immediately. The expansive network of tunnels and rooms carved into the limestone could be transformed into an impregnable hostel for clandestine activities. When Hans saw the site for the first time, he handed Itus blueprints and said, "Turn these tunnels into a fortress. Ensure no one but the three of us knows they exist."

Under Itus's direction, the caves were transformed into a self-contained facility with living quarters, kitchens, training rooms, and cells for captives. Outside the caves, a freshwater pool was created by redirecting natural streams. The pool served as both a utility and a symbol of Itus's authority over nature and man.

Three times a year, the caves became the center of intense activity. Orders placed months in advance by international clients were prepared for shipment. The "products," as the victims were called, were meticulously graded and groomed. Payment was required upfront, and those who failed to pay saw their orders disappear, their "products" discarded or repurposed for other uses. Rejection by a buyer could mean death for the captives, with the caves' guards and operatives indulging in unspeakable acts before disposal.

To keep the workforce compliant, Itus supplied them with a steady stream of hallucinogenic substances derived from local plants. The male recruits, often deemed expendable, were manipulated into submission through starvation, pain, and narcotics. These tactics ensured unwavering obedience, even in the face of the organization's horrifying demands.

Among the captives, there were those who stood out. Some young girls were kept for special assignments, trained to become recruiters for fresh victims. These were the elite, their education focused on manipulating others while maintaining their subservience to the syndicate.

During one of the infamous Piwari feasts, where guards celebrated before a shipment, the line between cruelty and camaraderie blurred. The rejected captives, deemed unfit for sale, were used as entertainment and then disposed of. The guards, emboldened by drugs and alcohol, reveled in their power over life and death. Itus watched from a distance, his face betraying no emotion as his two teenage sons participated in the macabre festivities. The boys, born to teenage captives and raised in the caves, were hardened in their father's image—cold, calculating, and devoid of empathy.

Over time, the boys became indispensable to Itus. They were his protégés, skilled in the use of poisons, traps, and the dense jungle's natural hazards. They carried out their father's darkest orders without question, their loyalty cemented by the fear and brutality they had endured since birth.

One day, Hans Boea visited the caves and met the young men. He was impressed by their discipline and efficiency, comparing them to Itus himself. "They'll carry your legacy," Hans remarked. Itus nodded, pride flickering in his otherwise impassive eyes.

The operation expanded as demand grew. Hans Boea's international network thrived on secrecy and precision. From raw gemstones smuggled in hollowed-out timber to human trafficking orchestrated with chilling efficiency, every aspect was executed flawlessly. The caves, hidden from the world, became a hub for this empire of exploitation.

Mala, now 16, had become one of the most prized "products." Her natural grace and beauty, honed through years of conditioning,

115

captivated even the hardened operatives. Karl Joel, one of Itus's most trusted men, found himself drawn to her. For the first time, he felt something other than lust—a haunting desire to possess her in a way that transcended mere ownership. Yet, he knew the dangers of acting on this impulse. Mala had been reserved for an influential buyer, and any interference could bring catastrophic consequences.

As the next shipment approached, the cave buzzed with activity. The MV Samara 2, a vessel identical to its ill-fated predecessor, was scheduled to transport the cargo to international waters. Mala's fate was sealed—another cog in the relentless machinery of Hans Boea's empire.

But within Mala, a faint ember of defiance remained. Though her spirit had been battered and scarred, a flicker of humanity endured, waiting for a chance to reignite.

CHAPTER 23

Across the Atlantic Divide

The MV Samara 2 sailed silently across the Atlantic, its twin diesel engines humming with mechanical precision. This voyage was meticulously planned, as always, to evade detection. Its cargo—smuggled gemstones hidden within hollowed-out timber and human lives trapped below deck—was worth millions. For Hans Boea's empire, the stakes were always high, and failure was not an option.

The journey from the Tumuck Humuck estuary to the west coast of Africa was perilous but routine. The vessel's captain and crew had performed this route countless times, navigating the vast Atlantic with skill. However, as they neared the Angolan coast, a ripple of tension swept through the ship. Reports of increased naval patrols had reached Hans Boea's ears, prompting him to send an urgent warning: Proceed with extreme caution.

The crew knew what was at stake. Below deck, the "life cargo" of young girls and boys, handpicked and groomed for the highest bidders, remained eerily silent. Their movements were restricted, and they were fed just enough to keep them alive for the journey. Their fates lay in the hands of buyers in a world that valued their innocence as a commodity.

Two days from their destination, the calm of the sea was broken by the sharp crackle of the ship's radio. Four naval patrol vessels were approaching. The captain's face paled as he realized the gravity of the situation. There was no way to avoid the inevitable. The MV Samara 2 was ordered to stop and prepare for inspection.

The French naval officers were thorough. They demanded access to the ship's manifest and cargo hold. On the surface, everything appeared legitimate—timber, rice, and other export goods. But as the officers probed deeper, they discovered inconsistencies. The hollowed-out timber revealed gemstones, and the rice bags contained concealed compartments of high-grade narcotics.

The ship was seized, and its crew detained for questioning. Interpol had been tipped off, though the source of the information remained unknown. The news reached Hans Boea within hours, courtesy of his informants embedded in various governmental agencies. The bust was a significant financial blow, but Hans's mind was already racing with plans to minimize the damage and shift attention away from his operation.

For Hans, the loss of the Samara 2 was a temporary setback, but it carried deeper implications. He called an emergency meeting with his key operatives, including Kurt Shalim and Itus. The tone of the meeting was tense. Hans's icy demeanor concealed the firestorm brewing within.

"This is a disruption, but it is not the end," Hans began, his voice calm yet menacing. "The network will adapt. The weak links will be identified and removed."

Kurt and Itus exchanged glances, understanding the subtext. The Samara 2's failure could not be entirely blamed on external forces. There had to be a mole or a breach in the chain of command. Hans's empire thrived on secrecy and precision; any deviation was intolerable.

Back at the Akari caves, Itus received a private summons from Hans. The conversation was blunt and unforgiving.

"Reinforce your operations," Hans ordered. "And ensure there are no more errors. If this happens again, I will not spare you."

Itus nodded, his face betraying no emotion. Deep down, however, he felt the weight of Hans's words. A single misstep could lead to his demise, along with the empire he had painstakingly built.

In a secluded location far from prying eyes, Kurt Shalim convened a meeting of his trusted associates. Among them was Karl Goel, who had quickly risen through the ranks due to his sharp mind and unwavering loyalty—or so Kurt believed. The group discussed strategies to tighten operations and mitigate risks, but Kurt couldn't shake the growing unease in his gut. The recent events had exposed vulnerabilities in their network, and he suspected that betrayal lurked within their ranks.

Karl Goel listened attentively, his face a mask of calm. As the meeting concluded, Kurt approached him.

"Stay vigilant, Karl," Kurt said, placing a hand on his shoulder. "I trust you to handle the critical assignments."

Karl nodded, offering a faint smile. "Of course, Mr. Shalim. You can count on me."

But as Kurt turned away, Karl's expression hardened. Deep within him, a plan was taking shape—one that would upend everything Kurt and Itus had built.

The green-painted military chopper hovered over the endless evergreen canopy like an insignificant mosquito, descending with precision to the edge of the beach where the receding tide had exposed a fresh stretch of compact, sugar-brown real estate.

Kurk Shalim, like a father guiding a trusted son, walked slowly up the sand dune with Carl Goel by his side. "Tell Itus I need to see him soon," he whispered into Carl's right ear.

"I will," Carl replied calmly—his left hand emerging from beneath his raincoat.

Shalim barely caught the glint of the army-issued 9mm automatic pistol in Carl's hand before the muffled shot rang out. The impact hurled him sideways, his body crashing onto its back, brains scattered in a gruesome halo beneath his shoulders. His lifeless eyes stared blankly at the dark clouds racing across the southern sky.

Without a flicker of emotion, Carl Goel stepped over the sand dune as the first drops of rain began pelting down like pilots descending from the heavens. Boarding the chopper, he turned to the pilot. "East," he commanded.

Karl had never been one to waste words or time—always a project, always a plan. And yet, watching him now, Van Cruni thought to himself, "He almost looks human."

The crisp Atlantic breeze carried the salty scent of corrida leaves through the tangled canopy above the avenue that led to a fork in the road. One narrow beam of sunrise began to conquer the foggy remnants of the night. Van Cruni's silver-grey SUV glided through the smoky mist, a sleek blur against the pale morning haze. Parked quietly along the dew-slicked, burnt-earth pathway was Kurt Shalim's black Humvee. His two bodyguards stood at attention beside their nearly identical vehicle, facing Van Cruni's from across the narrow trail.

Inside the Humvee, a figure sat reading something on his phone, his silhouette barely visible through the tinted, mist-covered window. Van Cruni stepped out of his SUV and approached. A few words were exchanged at the driver's side before he turned and walked back toward his vehicle.

As he neared the bodyguards, Van Cruni offered a wry glance. "You two following me?" The words had barely left his lips before he saw the cold, hollow barrel of a 9mm semi-automatic pointed at his chest.

The sharp crack of gunfire tore through the misty quiet. Six startled Canji pheasants burst into flight, their wings slicing the damp air, vanishing into the clumps of swamp-side cedar trees.

Both vehicles started with a low purr, then reversed, calmly driving away down the path they had come.

Van Cruni's lifeless eyes remained fixed, wide in terror, the sound of the final explosion etched into his vacant expression. A single red dot marked his forehead—behind it, the back of his skull had been obliterated, fragments of greyish, gelatinous brain matter staining the wet green grass. His dark red blood seeped into the scorched earth, its color nearly indistinguishable from the soil itself.

Meanwhile, in the Angolan port where the Samara 2 was impounded, authorities were celebrating their victory. The bust was one of the largest in recent history, and the media frenzy ensured that it became an international headline. However, the human cargo had yet to be discovered. The secret compartments holding the young captives remained hidden, a testament to Hans Boea's ingenuity.

For now, the young lives below deck were safe from discovery, but their journey was far from over. Somewhere in the shadows, Hans Boea's network was already moving to recover its assets and silence any loose ends.

CHAPTER 24

The Rise and Fall of Kuresh

Kuresh Laura, Blanka Smith, and Akash Reeds grew up in the rugged mining camp of Lidamine Creek, nestled between the Eastern Rupununi and the western tips of the Berbice River. Their friendship, forged in the harsh environment of Guyana's interior, had endured through the years. From childhood games in the dense rainforest to shared struggles as young adults, their bond was unbreakable.

By the time they reached adulthood, the trio found themselves adrift, their dreams battered by the grim realities of their surroundings. They scavenged for odd jobs in the bustling fishing and sugarcane industries but found little more than frustration and poverty. As desperation mounted, they turned to petty crime—a path that eventually led to their arrest. Their reckless antics landed them as reluctant guests in a government facility, serving two-year sentences for theft.

Kuresh, always the most daring of the three, quickly became a natural leader. His charisma and bravado often masked a darker, calculating mind. He thrived in adversity, earning the grudging respect of the guards and his fellow inmates alike. His escape plan—an audacious leap over the fence during a transfer to the magistrate's court—was the stuff of local legend. His success in eluding the authorities inspired whispers of admiration among the prisoners and villagers alike.

Kuresh's escape took him across the Corentyne River, where he found refuge in a remote fishing community. With a mix of cunning and hard work, he earned a place among the local fishermen. These men, too, had their secrets—refugees and outlaws seeking anonymity on the wide open waters of the Atlantic.

Kuresh quickly established himself as an indispensable member of the community. His sharp mind and natural charisma allowed him to navigate the social dynamics of the group. He soon owned his first fishing boat and employed other desperate men, creating a small but loyal crew.

In time, Kuresh's ambitions extended beyond fishing. He began smuggling goods across the porous borders, exploiting the lack of enforcement. His growing influence caught the attention of his employer, a seasoned fisherman with an eye for business. The older man, wary of Kuresh's criminal past, was initially reluctant to trust him. But over time, Kuresh's diligence and dedication softened the older man's stance. Eventually, Kuresh caught the eye—and the heart—of the man's daughter, Kamil.

Their courtship was anything but traditional. Kuresh, eager to prove himself worthy, worked tirelessly to earn the family's approval. Over time, his persistence paid off. He married Kamil, securing not only her love but also a legitimate foothold in the fishing industry. This marriage marked a turning point in Kuresh's life, solidifying his place in the community and providing the legal status he needed to thrive.

Kuresh's business grew rapidly. He expanded his fleet and began coordinating fishing operations for other locals, leveraging his connections to create a thriving enterprise. His boats brought in bountiful catches, which he sold to exporters in Europe and Asia. The profits were staggering, and Kuresh soon became one of the wealthiest men in the region.

But with success came new challenges. The government, struggling to manage an influx of illegal immigrants and burgeoning fishing operations, began implementing stricter regulations. Licenses were required to operate fishing boats, and compliance became a costly affair. Kuresh, ever resourceful, found ways to navigate these obstacles. He used bribes and forged documents to secure licenses for his fleet, ensuring his operations remained above suspicion.

His influence extended beyond the fishing docks. Kuresh became a key figure in the local community, helping to fund schools and provide jobs for struggling families. His philanthropic efforts earned him respect and loyalty, but they also masked the darker side of his empire.

Despite his outward respectability, Kuresh's empire was built on a foundation of crime. His boats were not just used for fishing; they also carried smuggled goods, including narcotics and contraband, across international waters. His connections to criminal networks ran deep, and his past associates began to resurface, seeking a piece of his success.

The influx of new fishing boats, fueled by foreign investments and government subsidies, threatened to disrupt the delicate balance of the industry. Rivalries emerged, and tensions between competing camps escalated. Kuresh, determined to maintain his dominance, resorted to intimidation and sabotage to protect his interests.

Over the years, Kuresh and Kamil had three sons, each inheriting their father's drive and ambition. The eldest, Jan, joined the military and quickly rose through the ranks, becoming a respected commander. His younger brothers followed similar paths, joining the police force and using their positions to protect their family's interests.

Kuresh's influence extended through his sons, who leveraged their authority to suppress rivals and secure lucrative deals for their father's enterprise. The family's reach grew, encompassing not only fishing but also real estate, shipping, and exports.

As Kuresh's empire flourished, whispers of discontent grew louder. Rivals who had been pushed aside began to plot their revenge. Former allies, resentful of Kuresh's success, looked for ways to undermine him. The government, increasingly wary of his growing power, began to scrutinize his operations more closely.

Kuresh, ever the strategist, knew he could not afford to let his guard down. The shadows of his past and the enemies he had made loomed large, threatening to unravel everything he had built.

CHAPTER 25

Of Fire and Blood: A Legacy of Greed

The couple sat quietly on the wooden swing beneath the elevated house. The steady rhythm of rain against the wide cotton hammock tied to a sprawling mango tree in the backyard filled the air. The swing creaked as it swayed gently, suspended by two sturdy chains fastened to the crossbeam of the floor above. Kamil leaned against her lover, listening to the storm's cadence.

"You'll have very little time to sleep, sweetheart," Kamil said softly, her voice tinged with concern. "This rain is going to last all night."

As if affirming her statement, a flash of lightning illuminated the neighborhood, followed by the deafening crash of thunder. The storm's fury startled the stray dogs, sending them scurrying for shelter under the swing.

"We should find a place to hide too," Kuresh replied with a wry smile.

"I'm no stray dog," Kamil teased, but her voice carried a trace of unease. She nestled closer to him, seeking warmth and reassurance.

"Shh," Kuresh whispered, his tone more commanding than comforting. He kissed her forehead, pulling her into his strong embrace. For a moment, they found solace in each other amidst the storm's chaos.

Kuresh rode his motorbike through the downpour without protective gear, the rain soaking him to the bone. The crash-shell road had turned to mush, and muddy puddles splattered his boots as he sped toward the waterfront shack. When he arrived, the boss's boat had not yet returned. Kuresh's lips curled into a faint, knowing smile.

"I hope they never return," he muttered under his breath.

The tide had receded, leaving the mudflats exposed. No other boats had returned either, but Kuresh anticipated their delay. He entered his shack, changed into dry clothes, and switched on his pocket radio. The crackling sound of static soon gave way to the soothing strains of an Indian melody, masking the sound of rain drumming against the zinc roof. Confident that his plan was foolproof, Kuresh allowed himself to relax, quickly drifting off to sleep.

"Kuresh! Wake up!" The frantic banging on the door jolted him awake.

"What is it?" he growled, his voice heavy with annoyance. "What's all this noise?"

"Something happened to the boss," a fisherman exclaimed, his face pale and drenched from the rain. "Last night, we saw a big ball of fire in the direction of the seine."

Kuresh feigned concern, rubbing his eyes as though trying to make sense of the news. "It must have been an engine problem. That Yamaha was new, though. Strange…"

Another fisherman chimed in, "The tide's out. It'll be six hours before any boat can leave the dock. We have a bad feeling about this, Kuresh."

Ever the opportunist, Kuresh took charge of the situation, barking orders with authority. "Form search parties. Each group will take a different section of the flats. The rest of you, keep processing yesterday's catch. We'll head out as soon as we can."

The search party found the seine tangled and half-buried in the mud, laden with fish. The boat and its crew were nowhere to be seen. "Empty the nets and hang them on the poles," Kuresh instructed. "We'll search the tree line."

Hours later, they recovered the charred remains of two human skeletons buried in the muck. By the time the tide rose, the police had arrived and placed the remains in body bags. Kuresh maintained his facade of grief, consoling Kamil and her mother as they sobbed uncontrollably.

"I'm so worried for Dad," Kamil whispered, clutching Kuresh's arm.

"We'll find out what happened," Kuresh assured her, his voice steady but detached.

In the wake of the tragedy, Kuresh married Kamil, cementing his status within the community. The marriage not only granted him legitimacy but also gave him access to the wealth and assets of his late father-in-law. Within weeks, Kuresh began expanding the family's fishing business, employing his old criminal connections to build a sprawling empire.

But the whispers began almost immediately. Some questioned the circumstances surrounding the fire, while others speculated about the fate of the boss and his assistant. Kuresh silenced dissent with bribes and intimidation, ensuring that the official narrative—a tragic accident at sea—was the only version of events.

As Kuresh's empire grew, so did his need for control. He monopolized the fishing industry in the region, securing licenses and concessions through a network of bribes and forged documents. His fleet expanded rapidly, outpacing rivals and drawing the attention of both the government and criminal organizations.

But success came at a cost. Rivals who dared to challenge him faced sabotage and ruin. Fishermen who resisted his authority found their boats mysteriously destroyed. Even within his inner circle, loyalty was enforced through fear, and betrayal was met with swift, merciless retribution.

Kuresh's past, once buried beneath layers of respectability, began to resurface. Old enemies and forgotten debts loomed on the horizon, threatening to dismantle the empire he had so carefully built.

CHAPTER 26

Piracy, Politics, and the Corentyne Border

From #61 Village, 10 degrees east of north, lies the beginning of the Corentyne River, marking the eastern border of the Republic of Guyana. According to international democratic principles, when determining the boundary between two countries separated by a significant body of water, such as the Corentyne River, the border is typically placed in the middle of the deepest channel.

During the colonial era, authority for granting permits for logging, mining, and balata bleeding in the Upper New River Triangle fell under the Dutch administration. However, the Dutch played a minimal role in Robert Schomburgk's survey of the Corentyne River border. The New River Triangle, claimed by Surinam, was addressed at the Geneva Convention in 1962. This issue was further reinforced in 1967, during the presidency of L.F.S. Burnham, when the Guyana Defence Force (GDF) expelled Surinamese troops from the area

Neighborly disputes over borders often resurface, particularly when tensions arise with Venezuela. In the 1960s, political destabilization efforts during the pre-independence period were driven by foreign nations intent on maintaining control over Guyana's sugar, bauxite, and other investments.

For over half a century, Guyanese citizens have faced harassment in Surinam, even while conducting legal business. Incidents of piracy—including hijacked outboard engines, seized catches, and looted boats—have escalated. These acts of piracy drive small-scale fishermen to financial ruin. Without police patrol boats—since the last one, Tacoba, was wrecked decades ago—law enforcement can do little beyond taking incident reports. Despite fishermen's pleas for protection from Surinamese authorities, piracy persists, with boats, nets, and engines ransomed while crews are left adrift in derelict vessels.

Like sharks circling a shoal of sardines, pirates have grown increasingly aggressive. Initially, outboard engines were their primary target, but now entire catches, food supplies, and tools are stolen. Despite the Corentyne River's extensive fishing fleet, its exportable catch has shown minimal growth.

At #43 Village near the Black Bush drainage outlet, Captain Burnett "Bodo" and his crew—Imtiaz, Rayman, Kutcher, Chubby, and Wayne—were preparing for another fishing trip aboard the Miss Otto. The boat, a 50-foot wooden, outboard-driven craft, was stocked and ready. Over the past five days, the crew had mended their nets under the shade of a sprawling mango tree near the shallow drainage canal.

The location was chosen for its proximity to the fishing grounds, saving on fuel costs. At low tide, the canal was little more than a trickle, but at high tide, the boats could safely cross the mudbanks and reach the ocean's deeper waters. Repairs to the net were necessary after their last trip, during which 800 blackfin sharks had damaged the mesh in their attempts to escape.

The Corentyne shoreline, enriched by silt deposits from the Orinoco, Essequibo, and Demerara Rivers, is a fertile feeding ground for species such as yellow catfish and gillbaka. The nutrient-rich waters, a blend of fresh and brine, create an ideal habitat for marine life. Over time, yellow catfish has become a cultural staple, enjoyed locally and exported in various forms: fresh, frozen, dried, and smoked.

As midnight approached, Captain Bodo started the Miss Otto's 115 HP Evinrude engine. Gazing up at the star-filled sky, he remarked to Kutcher, "This is so good." When asked what he meant, Bodo replied, "The fresh salt air flowing through my hair makes me feel alive. I just love the sea."

Kutcher joked, "My wife says the sea is your first love, and she doesn't want to be your second wife. You spend more time at sea than at home!" The crew laughed, sharing camaraderie as they readied the boat for another journey.

Once in the open sea, they began casting their net. Captain Bodo explained the mechanics of fishing in the shallows versus deeper waters and the importance of sustainability. The crew discussed overfishing and the need for larger mesh sizes to protect smaller fish, demonstrating an increasing awareness of environmental responsibility.

The fishing trip was productive, but their work was interrupted by the arrival of five unfamiliar boats. Captain Bodo noted their purposeful approach and ordered his crew to cover the catch. To their surprise, one of the boats was captained by Graab, a former crew member of the Miss Otto. Graab, now part of a new fleet funded by a mysterious investor, reported that three inexperienced crew members had fallen overboard during a storm.

Despite their sympathy, the crew couldn't help but question the competence of these newly promoted captains. "Graab can't even tie a bowline knot," Wayne muttered, shaking his head in disbelief.

As the trip continued, the crew reflected on their blessings and the challenges of their profession. The Miss Otto returned to shore with a sensational haul—the most profitable of the year. The crew celebrated their success, but the discovery of the three lost fishermen's bodies served as a sobering reminder of the sea's dangers.

Wayne carefully released two young yellow catfish from the net, a gesture of sustainability that earned the approval of his crew. The men vowed to advocate for responsible fishing practices, recognizing that the ocean's resources must be preserved for future generations.

Captain Bodo concluded, "The sea is not just our livelihood—it's our legacy."

CHAPTER 27

Trials on the Corentyne: Piracy, Exploitation, and Resilience

Bunface, Hafiz Jin, Poliohead, and Smithy stood near the shoreline, their eyes fixed on the fishing boats dotting the horizon. Each had their own ideas on how to take advantage of the men working those crafts. After much discussion, they finally devised a plan, confident it would be foolproof.

Out on the Miss Otto, the icebox was almost full with a prime catch. The yellow catfish were particularly large, and the snapper and trout hauled in were well above average size.

"These gillbaka must weigh more than a hundred pounds each, Captain!" Rayman said cheerfully.

"That's more than your body weight," Wayne teased. "You need to stop guzzling all that bush rum and eat more of this fish!"

The crew laughed as Wayne continued to rib Rayman. "Three days ashore, and you're drunk every day. Where did you find him this time, Haresh?"

Haresh grinned knowingly. "Under Miss Mavis' rum table, right by the fence in her backyard. And guess what? He wasn't alone—a stray dog was kissing him!"

"Captain, don't mind them," Rayman chimed in. "If they laid down, even the gulls would fly away from the sound of their snoring!"

The laughter continued as Rayman shared how the owner of the Big Shark boat had tried to hire him, only to get upset when Rayman joked that the shark painted on the boat's hull scared the fish away.

"Okay, everyone," Captain Bodo finally said, smiling. "Get some rest. We'll start picking up the nets in three hours—rain or no rain."

The crew settled in as rain began to fall, drumming steadily on the Miss Otto's wooden planks. The thunderclouds overhead kept the waves low, and the gentle swells made for a comfortable rhythm. Captain Bodo leaned against a sack of rice, entering a half-sleep while keeping his ears tuned for any unusual sounds.

Unbeknownst to the crew, danger was closing in. A small paddle-powered balahoo approached silently, barely visible in the downpour. Three masked men slipped aboard the Miss Otto with practiced ease. The first warning came as two machetes slammed forcefully against the cabin's zinc walls, the sound ringing out like gunfire.

"All of you—come out with your hands in the air, or I'll chop them off!" boomed a menacing voice.

The crew froze in terror as the sound of blades striking the cabin walls continued, accompanied by shouted threats. Captain Bodo raised his hand to his lips, silently signaling his men to stay calm.

"Don't shoot, please—we're coming out!" Captain Bodo called out, carefully raising his hands as he emerged from the cabin. The hijackers wasted no time, binding his hands tightly behind his back and shoving him roughly into the empty seine pen.

"Bend your f***ing head! What are you looking at?" one pirate snarled, driving a knee into Bodo's stomach. He collapsed, gasping for air, before a vicious kick rendered him unconscious.

Haresh was the next to emerge, his shoulder accidentally bumping one of the hijackers. The man staggered momentarily but quickly recovered, pulling a concealed ice pick from his waistband. Without hesitation, he drove it into Haresh's chest with brutal force. Haresh fell into the water, his body sinking silently beneath the waves.

Wayne, regaining consciousness, tried to stand but was immediately beaten with the wooden handle of a machete. "Please, sir, don't hurt me! I can't breathe!" he begged, tears streaming down his face.

"Shut up, or I'll cut your tongue out!" the pirate yelled, slamming the butt of his shotgun into Wayne's midsection. Wayne crumpled to the floor, unconscious once more.

The remaining crew members were forced out of the cabin, trembling as they faced the pirates' wrath. Rayman and Kutcher were struck with pistol butts and machete handles, their screams of pain lost in the pounding rain. Intiaz was hit with the flat side of a cutlass, the blow knocking him off balance. Another strike sent him overboard, disappearing into the water like Haresh.

The pirates tied the remaining men's hands behind their backs and gagged them with pieces of Styrofoam. Forcing them into the balahoo, the pirates taunted their victims. "Count yourselves lucky! Go home—if you survive!"

The rain continued to fall, erasing any evidence of the brutal attack.

In the balahoo, Captain Bodo, battered but conscious, urged his crew to paddle with the wooden benches they managed to salvage. "We're not far from shore," he said, his voice weak but determined.

Hours later, they reached the sandy beach and made their way to the nearest public road. A passing minibus took them to a police station ten miles away, where they reported the attack.

The next day, news spread that six other boats had been robbed that night. Five fishermen had lost their lives, their bodies recovered from the river and nearby mudflats. The Miss Otto's crew had survived, but the attack left them physically and emotionally scarred.

Captain Bodo suffered fractured ribs, a concussion, and a dislocated shoulder, requiring two weeks of hospitalization. Wayne, with severe internal injuries, spent two months recovering. The other crew members, overwhelmed by trauma, left the fishing trade entirely.

Despite police investigations and brief detentions of suspects, including Poliohead and Smithy, no charges were brought due to lack of evidence. The attacks continued sporadically, leaving the fishing community in fear. For many, the scars—both physical and emotional—would never fully heal.

Years later, families of the lost fishermen continued to wait, gazing at the horizon in the faint hope that their loved ones might somehow return.

Meanwhile, competition for fishing grounds on the Corentyne intensified. Overcrowded waters, tangled nets, and overfishing strained the industry. The arrival of foreign conglomerates further complicated matters, as unsupervised logging and fishing operations exploited the region's resources.

Amid these challenges, the fishermen of the Corentyne struggled to protect their livelihood, knowing that the river and the ocean were both their greatest resource and their greatest risk.

CHAPTER 28

Lines of Power: The Corruption Behind the Nets

Invitations were extended by local officials to neighboring fishing and security personnel. The purpose was to address the status of rumored activities in the region—an opportunity not to be missed. The invitations were accepted, and a team of visitors arrived. Discussions ensued, focusing on safety measures for fishermen, but no official agreements were reached, as the meeting had not been sanctioned through diplomatic channels.

Across the border, the approach to these issues was markedly different, reflecting a national seriousness that was absent locally. "What did your visit across the border reveal?" the chairman began, setting the tone for the unofficial debrief. "What are the developments in their fishing industry? Where are their markets, and how much do they earn? Did you gather details on their boats, the size of their nets, or their military installations?"

The first speaker summarized his observations. "There are more fishing boats than we could count. At one ice facility alone, about 200 crafts were beached on the mudbank during low tide, with hundreds more reportedly at sea," he said, shaking his head in disbelief before introducing the next speaker.

"In most of the boats I inspected, there was no visible safety equipment. The cramped cabins—barely 12 by 8 feet, with only one escape hatch—are death traps. And yet, men live in these conditions for weeks, storing hundreds of gallons of gasoline while navigating rough seas. There is no control over the length of nets, the size of the gauge, or the species caught. It's essentially a free-for-all.

"Licenses displayed on the boats are often fake, with duplicates of a single original. While many of the crafts are seaworthy, the same cannot be said for their crews. Most are untrained, undocumented, and lack proper identification. Among them are failed farmers, school dropouts, and retirees from various trades. Few, if any, have any background in deep-sea fishing."

The speaker concluded, and another official added, "There seems to be a complete disconnect between the central authority and the regional groups. In my opinion, this entire fleet is financed by foreign investors. Local financial institutions are unwilling to insure fishing equipment, which means these operations are essentially unregulated."

The frustration in the room was palpable. "Nothing we've tried has stopped them from exploiting our fish stocks!" one man exclaimed. "And now their authorities have the audacity to demand that we grant legitimacy to these people while they pillage our waters!"

A senior official intervened. "This is why we're here," he said firmly. "Put your teams to work immediately."

146

Kuresh Sr., newly promoted as the chief security officer for the northern district, was instructed to take action. The regime's grip on the security forces was ironclad, with special units created to enforce obedience and monitor illegal activities. These units extorted, blackmailed, and exploited their targets, often enriching themselves in the process.

Kuresh Jr., rising quickly within the ranks, became notorious for his wealth and cruelty. He flaunted his fortune in casinos, clubs, and among his peers, while using his power to terrorize the community. "I keep my daughter hidden whenever he's around," one father whispered. "The girls in this neighborhood fear him like a disease."

The fishing villages, meanwhile, thrived economically. Their consistent catches of exportable species generated significant foreign exchange. Fishing equipment, once scarce, became abundant, with outboard engines sold to loggers and miners. But the origins of this wealth were dubious. "These outboards have no serial numbers," one buyer remarked to a mechanic. "That's why you're getting them at half the price," the mechanic replied dismissively, pocketing his payment.

Concerns about security escalated as reports surfaced of illegal trawlers operating on the Atlantic shelf. Satellite images revealed a massive fish-processing factory about 200 miles offshore, pillaging resources without oversight. "The destruction of our fish stocks and habitats is catastrophic," the Navy commander declared in a private meeting with Kuresh Sr.

The commander, employing a mix of intimidation and manipulation, pressed Kuresh Sr. to act. "Your family's wealth and privileges are tied to this country's generosity. Now is the time to prove your loyalty," he said coldly. "You've taken boats, engines, and nets, yet their fleet only grows larger. Show that you are worthy of the trust we've placed in you, and you will be protected from any repercussions."

Kuresh Sr., feeling cornered, reflected on the circle of crime that had defined his life. His wealth, amassed through corruption, had secured his son's rise to power and brought a veneer of legitimacy to their operations. But now, that same system was calling in its debts.

Kuresh Jr.'s rise in the military was fueled by financial contributions to his superiors. His hatred for his father's former countrymen was well-known, driven by the lies of criminals who had found refuge in their fishing enterprise. His charisma and brutality made him both a leader and a figure of fear among his men.

The orders were clear: stop the illegal activities and demonstrate loyalty to the regime. Kuresh Sr. assembled a team of trusted enforcers, men trained in violence and survival, to carry out the mission. "There must be no failure," he told them. "Protect your identities with your lives."

The group, led by hardened veterans Hanked Mugo and Roya Abea, prepared for their task with ruthless determination. The stage was set for a confrontation that would test the limits of loyalty, greed, and survival on the turbulent waters of the Corentyne.

CHAPTER 29

The Call of the Deep: Survival and Sacrifice

Page Bin, Kudari Mike, Square Hooknose, Dasrat Dagman, and Captain Muckdeo sailed out from Port #66 aboard the *Big Trout*. The vessel, recently repainted navy blue and red, was powered by a new 75 HP Yamaha outboard motor. With its icebox packed with six tons of crushed ice, they prepared for a two-week fishing trip, despite the scarce catches of the past three months.

Nearby, the crew of the *Phantom*—Indo Prem, Nigel Gilry, Thonny, Longhead, and Jinger Foot—readied their vessel under the leadership of Captain Big Boy. Meanwhile, Mr. Shaz Abdin, owner of two hill-net boats, addressed his men.

"There's a new export market opening up. They're paying better and even buying second-grade fish for sun-drying at a plant being set up along the shoreline. They'll be here in twelve days, and if we can supply enough to make their venture profitable, they'll stay. If not, we'll lose them to our neighbors across the river. Good luck and stay safe."

With that, he climbed into his ton-ton center truck and left the #43 village port.

At Port #66, the *Snapper King* and *Ocean Queen* were grounded. Despite stocking ice and provisions two days earlier, their crews had indulged in a sprawling two-day drinking spree, draining their last week's earnings. Now sober, they scrambled to restock and prepare for a delayed departure during the night tide.

Captain Bigfoot James, skipper of the *Ocean Bucket*, had his own crew issues. He had fired two crew members, Keaton and Roy Kur, for extending their drinking binge and cursing him when he intervened.

"You two can find work elsewhere," Captain Bigfoot said firmly at Dolly's Watering Hole.

"Come on, Captain, have another beer, and we'll settle this!" pleaded Keaton Kur, throwing an arm around Bigfoot's shoulders.

"No. Maybe next trip—if you're sober," Bigfoot replied. "Your working bags will be left with the dock watchman."

Later, Captain Bigfoot handed the Kur brothers' belongings to the watchman. "If they come when sober, give them their stuff," he instructed.

The watchman, Mr. Francis, seized the opportunity. "Captain, my two brothers are out of work. They've worked at sea before and can join you now if you need replacements."

Relieved, Captain Bigfoot accepted the offer. The Francis brothers—Luke, 26, and Mat, 24—were skilled seamen and respected in their community. Married to twin sisters who had been their schoolmates, the brothers shared a strong Presbyterian faith, earning them the nickname "The Francis Disciples."

Their dedication to family was well known. "My boys take care of us, and their wives support them. Today, that's something to be proud of," their mother told a neighbor, who replied, "We elect leaders who promise to make us rich, yet our hospitals lack dialysis machines, and our farmers struggle to sell their produce.

As Captain Bigfoot James waited for the tide, he reflected on his life. "I'm 56 years old with three children in high school, a mother who needs daily insulin, and an aging father too frail to help around the house. After 40 years at sea, 30 as a captain, I'm stuck with rookies and drunkards," he thought, shaking his head.

Yet he saw potential in his crew. "They're good boys, desperate to make an honest living. They see me as a role model, teacher, and moral guide. It's a heavy responsibility," he mused before dozing off to the soothing rhythm of shallow waves.

When the tide finally rose, Captain Bigfoot's rival, Captain Jano Renzen of the *Snapper King*, was still ashore, his crew recovering from their drinking binge. Bigfoot seized the opportunity, pushing the *Ocean Bucket* into the deep channel.

"Our world has changed, and not for the better," Bigfoot lamented aloud. "I hate to leave friends behind, but in fishing, the first drop of the net can make or break us."

Captain Jacob Roy of the *Miss Pakiza* was frustrated. His crew had been chasing shoals of mullet for three tides without success. "Let's head east toward the shallow end of the mudflat," suggested Old Brown, a seasoned fisherman with fifty years of experience.

Captain Roy, humbled by his failure to follow Old Brown's earlier advice, agreed. "No offense taken, son," Old Brown said with a smile. "Every day is a fishing day, but not every day is a bonanza."

For Old Brown, the sea was a way of life. "The ocean is my addiction," he told the crew. "The breeze calms my spirit, the waves thrill me, and the fish fights give me a sense of conquest. Above all, I enjoy the company of brave sea bats like you."

Meanwhile, Mr. Tuku Ram, owner of the *Miss Daisy One* and *Miss Daisy Two*, lamented the difficulty of recruiting experienced fishermen. "Most seasoned men have joined new boats. The rest are inexperienced and undisciplined. There's no prestige in this work anymore," he said.

Captain Hazel of the *Sandaka* echoed these frustrations. "Two years ago, we filled our iceboxes in days. Now, hundreds of nets drag over the same stretch, and oil exploration has disrupted the ecosystem. My kids need books, clothes, and food. I hope for a reasonable catch to cover expenses," he said.

As the tides turned, four wooden boats modified for speed and maneuverability emerged from hidden channels along the muddy shoreline. Each was equipped with dual 225 HP Yamaha outboards. Masked men in marine camouflage loaded the crafts with heavy bags.

The crews, strangers to each other, were carefully chosen for their specific skills. The mission, shrouded in secrecy, offered a chance for redemption. Under the cover of darkness, the boats sped into the rough waters, each heading in a different direction like black wasps buzzing toward an uncertain fate.

CHAPTER 30

The Price of the Deep

"It's time to line up the seine, boys! Darkness will be upon us in two hours. We'll start picking up at 10 p.m.," Captain Mukdeo directed his crew.

"How do you know where we are, Captain?" Pagle Bin asked, mesmerized by the captain's ability to navigate in the dark.

"I use the stars," Captain Mukdeo replied casually, more focused on ensuring the net was cast correctly. "Once we're finished throwing the seine, I'll point it out to you," he added, ever eager to teach his men when the opportunity arose.

"The sun's going down so fast, it's as if it's hiding from the night," Square Head remarked, his tone reflective.

"All of you, get some rest. I'll wake you when it's time," the captain instructed, steady and composed.

Meanwhile, a speeding craft skimmed across the waves like a flying fish, heading toward the faint lamplight on the stern of the *Big Trout*. The sound of its outboard engines was muffled by wet jute bags draped over their hoods. As the vessel approached, it appeared as if the fishing boat lay empty, tied loosely to a long polythene rope.

With the agility of a monkey leaping through trees, two masked men armed with AK-47s and cutlasses jumped into the empty net pen of the *Big Trout*. The cabin erupted into chaos as the deafening explosions of gunfire shattered the quiet night.

"Shut the f…k up!" snarled one of the bandits. A third figure leaped aboard, carrying a heavy duffel bag in one hand and a double-barrel shotgun in the other.

"Come out with your hands in the air, or I'll chop them off!" he bellowed.

One by one, the terrified crew emerged. Captain Mukdeo raised his hands as they shot up through the cabin's bench entrance. A bandit roughly zipped a broad plastic tie over the captain's clasped wrists, pulling it tight with cruel efficiency.

Captain Mukdeo screamed as the tie cut into his skin. Without hesitation, the bandit slammed the butt of his AK-47 into the captain's nose, sending him crumpling to the floor, blood pouring from the wound.

"Stay down! Turn on your belly, or I'll put a slug through your stupid skull!" the bandit barked, kicking Mukdeo's side as he struggled to comply.

Each crew member was treated with equal brutality. The third bandit pulled six pairs of iron shackles from his duffel bag, each connected by heavy, short chains. Working like men possessed, they shackled the fishermen's feet and left them sobbing quietly on the deck.

The bandits then grabbed Captain Mukdeo by his chains, one lifting his feet and the other his hands. Without hesitation, they heaved him overboard into the dark waters. The splash was barely audible over the rhythm of the waves.

One by one, the crew followed their captain into the sea, their shackles sealing their fate.

Satisfied with their monstrous work, the bandits surveyed the boat. Finding no one else, they cut the seine tie, sending the fishing craft adrift. The *Big Trout* swung helplessly into the waves as the bandits sped eastward, disappearing into the night.

Six miles east, the crew of the *Phantom* was pulling in their seine. The first quarter mile of net yielded a dozen 17-pound gray snappers and an equal number of blackfin sharks.

"Longhead, you and Johnny start icing the catch," Captain Big Boy instructed. "Use the floodlight to make sure you cut the fins properly and save the eggs and swim bladders of the snapper," he added.

Unbeknownst to the *Phantom*, a speeding craft approached in the shadows, the low sound of its engine muffled by the natural noise of the waves.

"They can't see us," one masked man whispered to his accomplice. "The floodlights blind them to anything beyond their boat."

The dark shape of the craft suddenly loomed beside the *Phantom* like a whale surfacing. A masked man leveled his shotgun and fired, the blast instantly killing Captain Big Boy. The force sent his body flying backward into the sea.

Indo Prem and Nigel Gilry, driven by instinct, dove into the waves. Their plunge sent them deep beneath the surface, but as they struggled upward for air, their hands and feet became ensnared in the taut polythene net. Kicking and thrashing only tightened the grip, and their fight for survival ended in silence as their bodies stilled beneath the waves.

Back on the boat, the remaining crew members were zip-tied together, their hands bound behind their backs and linked by short lengths of polythene rope. The bandits beat them mercilessly before throwing them overboard like discarded waste.

The *Phantom*, its deck bloodied and empty, was left to drift, another victim of the lawless waters.

CHAPTER 31

The Corentyne's Dark Waters: Piracy, Survival, and Loss

At the Mahaica River fisheries port, a crew comprising Guinea Bird, Piglet Thief, Mustafa, Freddy Anson, and Jacob Silverstein, led by Captain Bunbury Bunsuga, waited for the tide to rise high enough to cross the mud reef at the estuary.

"It'll be deep enough by sundown for us to cross," the captain assured them as they sat under the shade of a sprawling courida tree.

"I always enjoy looking out at the far blue horizon over the calm water from here," Guinea Bird remarked, seemingly lost in admiration of the sea's serene beauty.

"Oh, you'll be riding high waves soon enough to reach where you're gazing," Mustafa teased, well aware of Guinea Bird's unease in rough seas.

"Well now, what business does a Guinea Bird have in the ocean anyway?" Piglet Thief joked.

"Look who's talking," Guinea Bird shot back mockingly, to the laughter of the crew.

Their boat, *Miss Nirvana*, was equipped with a mile-long seine net and all the necessary accessories. Captain Bunbury Bunsuga set their departure plan. "We'll reach the fishing grounds by eight tonight, just across the Corentyne River. By ten, under the glittering stars, we'll start casting the net across the mudflat," he said with confidence.

The captain shared news about a new Eastern market eager for quriman and high-water fish, explaining, "I hear these species respond very well to sun drying. If things work out as planned, this season's catch could set us all up financially."

The crew listened, some reflecting on their personal struggles. "Captain, I'm sorry it took us three or four days to get ready for this trip," Freddy Anson said apologetically. "Jacob and I were dealing with flooded rice fields. The rain last week was too much for the drainage."

"I hope the government gives us compensation," Jacob Silverstein added. "But I don't see farmers sticking with their fields much longer. No reliable markets and no support. It's a losing game."

Mustafa nodded in agreement. "My parents and grandparents were farmers. Back then, the marketing board bought crops and sold them overseas for foreign exchange. Now the government is selling gold concessions for pennies and cutting shady deals over timber and oil."

"Oil that's destroying the climate right next to the Amazon Forest," Piglet Thief interjected. "And for what? A tiny 2% cut while the oil companies make their profits. We're selling our future for peanuts."

The crew shared a laugh as Guinea Bird stumbled over the net, tangling himself in its loops. "Looks like the blind leading the posse!" he quipped as he tried to untangle himself.

As the crew joked and prepared, a black speedboat approached on the western horizon, its prow cutting through the waves like a ghost. The masked men aboard moved with cold precision, armed with AK-47s and a double-barrel shotgun.

Captain Bunbury Bunsuga and his crew, engrossed in their preparations, had no time to react. The crack of gunfire shattered the night as bullets tore through the boat. Captain Bunbury fell first, followed by the crew members who were struck down one by one.

Guinea Bird, splattered with blood and wounded, managed to feign death. When the pirates began tossing bodies overboard, he was among them, hitting the water silently, holding his breath, and sinking beneath the waves to stay out of sight.

Elsewhere, Captain Burgess Frank and his crew on the *Miss Challenger* were celebrating a lucrative trip. Each crew member had earned over $10,000 from their last haul. With spirits high, they prepared for another successful venture, planning to follow a shoal of blackfin sharks near Shell Beach.

The *Miss Challenger* crew had just begun their fishing operations when the black speedboat appeared. Like a predator stalking its prey, the pirates attacked with ruthless efficiency. The night erupted in violence as bullets tore through Captain Burgess Frank and his men. Only silence remained as their lifeless bodies were dumped into the sea.

On the *Miss Cassie*, Captain Harris Singh and his crew had been fishing successfully for ten days. Their icebox was half full, and they were eager to head home. As the crew exchanged jokes and anticipated their return, the black speedboat struck again.

Bullets rained down, leaving Captain Harris and his men lifeless on the deck. The pirates executed the survivors with chilling indifference, throwing their bodies overboard before cutting the boat free and speeding away into the night.

The waters of the Corentyne River were no longer just a livelihood for the fishermen. They had become a battleground, where piracy reigned unchecked, and dreams of a prosperous catch turned into a fight for survival. In the face of these atrocities, fear spread among the fishing community, leaving them to question how long they could endure these relentless attacks.

Chapter 32

The Tide Turns: Trials of the Anesa Fleet

The *Miss Anesa 1* and *Miss Anesa 2* had been fishing off the coast of the Copanama River estuary for four days. Each trawl covered about twenty miles westward, opposite the deep Caroni mudflats. Despite the rising spring tide increasing water speed, their efforts were beginning to yield a more promising variety of species.

"Fishing has always been a gamble," mused Captain Ravi Sen of the *Miss Anesa 1* as he worked with his crew to clear tangled yellow catfish from their nets. "Timing is everything." The trout in the haul were easier to untangle, having no external bones, and the crew worked with anticipation, hoping for a profitable trip after a slow start.

"Captain, this fishing ground seems overworked—too many competitors," remarked Little Boy in a respectful tone, voicing what many on the crew were thinking.

Captain Ravi nodded. "I'm open to suggestions. This is unlike any trip we've had before. By now, we'd usually be heading home with full ice boxes."

Hooknose, another crew member, chimed in, "When I worked with long-line boats, we used deep-sea trawling. It's worth considering, but it requires more equipment—rope, lead, and time—to adjust our nets for greater depths."

Acknowledging the challenge, Captain Ravi replied, "That's true. For now, we could head to the east bank of the Paramaribo River estuary. It's usually productive at this time of year, and our licenses allow us to fish there."

Little Boy perked up. "I've worked on boats based on the Paramaribo River. I still remember some of the good fishing spots."

Nearby, *Miss Anesa 2* was trawling to the north. Captain Pennux Petersburg and his crew had enjoyed moderate success, with the first three days yielding half a full icebox of valuable catch. However, the remaining days had brought smaller hauls.

"Do you think Captain Ravi and his crew are catching more than us?" asked deckhand Prince Jonathan, watching his companions prepare shark fins for drying.

"It's hard to say unless we can magically peek into their icebox," quipped CorkKnee Zaman, laughing. He mimicked a bird flapping its wings, making comical chicken noises, which sent the crew into fits of laughter.

Despite the humor, Captain Pennux remained pensive. "I was just thinking about how this is the only work most of us know how to do. Our families depend on us. Out here, it's not just about fishing—it's survival. But how long can we keep doing this if the catches don't improve?"

"I feel the same," added Fowl, one of the crew. "I don't want my kids to grow up thinking their father couldn't provide for them."

Later, *Miss Anesa 2* maneuvered alongside her sister craft, and the captains exchanged updates. "How's your catch going?" Pennux asked.

"Average," Ravi admitted. "We're heading to the morning market soon and might return for another trip. Anything you want me to tell the boss?"

Pennux nodded. "Let him know we'll stay out a bit longer. We're finally getting some decent catches now."

As the two boats parted, the crews exchanged friendly banter. "Hey, Hooknose! Don't drink all the El Dorado rum before we're back!" shouted one of the *Miss Anesa 2* crew members, sparking laughter.

Unbeknownst to the fishermen, danger lurked nearby. A dark speedboat, its engine muffled to a near whisper, was anchored behind the mudflats, hidden from view. The masked occupants watched the fishing boats intently, their eyes like predators stalking prey.

As *Miss Anesa 1* began casting its nets, the speedboat advanced under cover of darkness, closing the gap with calculated precision. The peaceful rhythm of the waves was shattered by chaos as the attackers boarded the fishing boat.

"Everyone down!" came a chilling command as the fishermen were overpowered and tied up. Cries of confusion and fear filled the air as their nets and equipment were ransacked. The attackers left the vessel adrift, vanishing as swiftly as they had appeared.

Captain Ravi's thoughts lingered on the challenges of their trade. "Between overfishing and these constant threats, it's a wonder we manage to survive out here at all," he reflected, steering his boat toward safer waters.

Meanwhile, the *Miss Anesa 2* had sailed farther along the estuary, its crew unaware of the looming danger. As they worked under the starry night, laughter and camaraderie filled the air, oblivious to the ominous silence beyond the horizon.

Chapter 33

Dark Tides: Stalking Shadows and the Fishermen's Struggle

The villages along Guyana's Atlantic coast, stretching from the Corentyne River to Georgetown, buzzed with grim whispers of catastrophe at sea. Boats, eerily empty, were spotted drifting past safety zones or lodged in the thick courida bushes lining the muddy coastline. Alarmed, local fishermen, families, and fisheries officials flooded police stations, urging immediate action for search and rescue operations.

As the tide began to reveal its grim secrets, bodies washed ashore—half-decomposed, grotesquely disfigured by fish and water, many barely recognizable. Some were found tangled in the roots of the courida trees, their mutilated forms bearing the unmistakable marks of torture. Families quickly buried the identified remains, while the unnamed victims were laid to rest in unmarked graves, their stories lost to the sea.

The horror of these killings made one thing abundantly clear: this was not about theft. The violence, marked by precision and cruelty, hinted at a deeper, more sinister motive.

"Shot to rob? Nonsense!" an enraged voice shouted at a gathering of fisheries officials. "Who uses AK-47s to kill unarmed fishermen? What are they trying to say—'Stay off the sea'? What is the government doing to protect us?" The cries of anger and despair grew louder, as grieving families, clutching their children, begged the police for answers. But the death toll only climbed, and closure remained elusive.

The anguish prompted desperate acts of solidarity among villagers. Some donated boats, fuel, and even firearms to aid in search efforts. Others crossed into neighboring Suriname to enlist the help of sympathetic officials. Still, the sorrow of missing loved ones hung heavy, with no solace in sight.

Finally, a faint glimmer of hope emerged. Guinea Bird, a survivor from the Miss Nirvana, was miraculously found alive. Clinging to a piece of Styrofoam dislodged during the attack, he had survived the treacherous waters. After washing up on the mud banks near Biggie Pond, he endured four harrowing days of wandering through snake-infested, mosquito-ridden swamps before a rice farmer discovered him. Barely alive, his body covered in cuts and leech bites, he was rushed to the hospital.

Guinea Bird's account of the nightmare aboard the Miss Nirvana sent shockwaves through the nation. His vivid descriptions of masked men, armed with AK-47s and machetes, confirmed what the mutilated bodies already suggested: these murders were calculated, professional, and meant to send a chilling message. Yet, despite collaborative efforts between Guyana and Suriname, the fate of dozens of missing men remained a mystery.

Amid the chaos, a single, cryptic phone call shattered the silence. Dialed to a secure line meant for one-time use, the caller uttered just two words: "Sever all leads." The line went dead, and the phone ceased to exist.

As the country mourned, Kuresh Jr. reveled in a very different world. An exclusive executive fête celebrated the nation's elite, with music, fine cuisine, and mingling opportunities for ambitious figures like Kuresh Jr. His flawless military uniform added to his aura of untouchability, his every move exuding confidence. The operation at sea, a secretive and sinister venture, had gone exactly as planned. The lack of feedback from his team, following protocol, only confirmed success.

"This mission deserves significant rewards," Kuresh Jr. thought smugly. "A promotion, overseas perks, unlimited travel expenses—it's all within reach." He basked in self-satisfaction, convinced his actions cemented his position among the ruling elite.

The following morning, the cool tropical breeze along the oceanfront felt like a blessing. Driving his jeep along a shell road, Kuresh Jr. admired the idyllic scenery. The night before had been one of indulgence, and he considered a dip in the black coal creek to cure his lingering hangover.

As he drove leisurely, a black Mercedes-Benz approached from the opposite direction. The vehicle's hood was rolled down, and Kuresh Jr. recognized his superior—a man he had hoped to impress at the casino party hours earlier. Slowing his jeep to exchange pleasantries, he prepared to greet the man.

Suddenly, a double-barreled shotgun erupted from the car's window. The blast obliterated the left side of Kuresh Jr.'s head, nearly severing it. His lifeless body slumped in the driver's seat as the jeep veered into tangled vines and plunged into a murky roadside trench.

The black Mercedes-Benz, now with its windows rolled up and air conditioning blasting, drove away without a trace. Its dark purpose, like the ocean's tide, left no trail behind.

ABOUT THE AUTHOR

Rabindra N. Prasad, aka "Taz"

Rabindra N. Prasad, affectionately known as "Taz," is an environmental advocate, commercial fisherman, educator, and storyteller shaped by the beauty and challenges of the Guyana Shield. Born under the majestic bamboo clumps at Jackson Creek, a remote area nestled on the western bank of the mighty Corentyne River, Taz's early life began in a humble 'Manicole Palm' benab built by his father in the shadows of the Amazon.

After completing his secondary and college education, Taz pursued a career as a science teacher, specializing in physics and environmental studies. However, his passion for the natural world extended beyond the classroom. His investments in fishing along the Atlantic coastline granted him unique insights into the struggles of fishermen battling poverty, piracy, and the relentless forces of nature in their pursuit of a livelihood from the sea.

Through these experiences, Taz witnessed the destructive forces of ignorance, greed, and lawlessness, which compounded the hardships of life along the Amazon. He saw firsthand how uncontrolled hunting, fishing, and logging devastated ecosystems, and how entire bird species were eradicated by poachers. At the same time, Taz's heart was with the fisherfolk—ordinary people who faced unspeakable losses from piracy, mourning fathers, brothers, and loved ones who perished in the unforgiving Atlantic, often with no grave or headstone to honor their memory.

Taz's life is a testament to resilience and purpose. He uses his experiences and stories to advocate for environmental conservation, sustainable practices, and justice for marginalized communities. Whether through his writing or his work on the water, Taz is dedicated to raising awareness, honoring the forgotten, and inspiring future generations to live in harmony with the natural world.

PHOTO GALLERY

And

LETTERS FROM THE TOUR MEMBERS

A typical fishing boat powered by an outbound engine carries nearly three miles of gill-net drift seine, neatly packed in the middle. The center bench supports the blue ice box, with styrofoam floats and visible flags stored nearby. The front deck, sheathed for protection, covers the cabin, while gasoline is securely stored under the shed at the rear of the vessel.

The framing of sixty three feet, twelve feet high by ten feet wide, gill-net fishing craft. Constructed on the West Bank of the Corentyne River.

Typical long boats used to access creeks or conduct repairs on pirate ships. These boats are paddle or oar driven for silence.

Early misty morning on the sparse vegetation of
the large sugar brown sand bay at Iguana Island
upper Corentyne River. Hundreds of colorful
butterflies gather on the sands.

179

The author TAZ and river guide preparing
night camp on one of the Islands in the
Governor Falls area - upper Corentyne River

Typical Jogging trash camp in the Sipolwini area made from concrete and manicole palm. Skillfully intertwined to produce a rainfall dry dwelling.

The author TAZ Demostrating the ease of hooking Red-Eye Pirana that infests the upper reachs of the Akari rapids.

The author walking on the shallow sand bar in pirana infested coffee black water. "Ura-Bank" upper Corentyne River below Warakabra Falls.

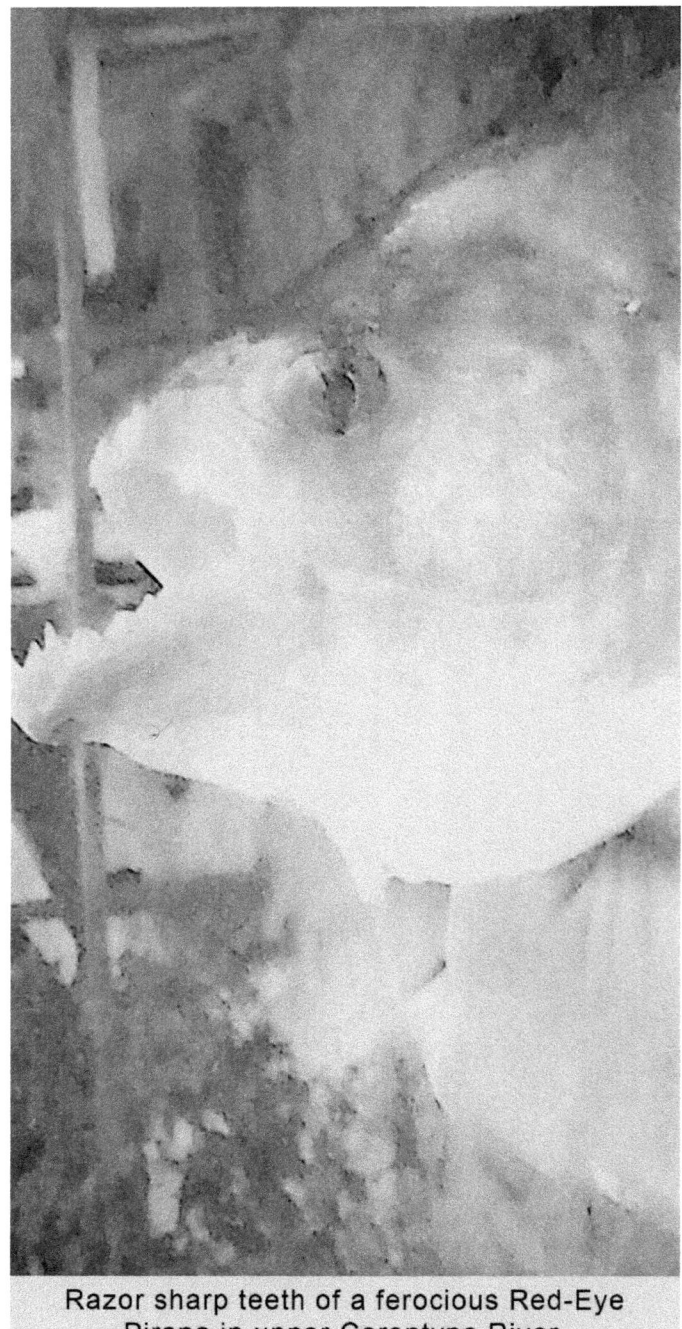

Razor sharp teeth of a ferocious Red-Eye
Pirana in upper Corentyne River.

To Alfred Salerno,

My special Home Depot friend, who has lent his artistic skills to help create the cover theme of this book's genius.

Thank you,
Rabindra Prasad

———————————

Taz brings heartfelt memories of a vanishing culture and a keen sense of injustice to telling the stories of a little-known corner of Guyana. His story is absorbing and sometimes tragic. You'll come away with respect for a people struggling to make a living from the jungle and the sea.

— Doug Meurs

———————————

Corantine 10-07 '93

This whole trip was an splendid organized expedition. The three people who put it together namely: Taxa, Regi and Roy went beyond themselves to make this trip come true.

I only can speak for myself, but I can tell you that I enjoyed every moment of it. We left Nw Nickerie on the 2nd of July en drove up the Corantine River until we reached the Wonotobo-falls, which we reached on the 5th of July.

Half of the members stayed there while the rest went further in an attempt to reach the King Frederick II falls, which they unfortunately because of a lack of time didn't succeed accomplished.

As I was a member of the group that stayed behind I filled my days with fishing, and bading in the falls, hunting and relaxing.

The greatest thing of staying in the bush is that people don't bother you on telefon, you don't have no newspapers on tv and your away from all your patients. I love it !!!

I only regret it that we have to turn and go back to civilization.

As my uncle Cyriel said I'm glad of being away from the bussines and hamering at home. (His house is being renovated)

Members of the group saw deer and alligators they even heard buffalo's

As I said before I love the life in the bush !

Harold Li Fo Sjoe
Cyriel Jong Tjien Fa

186

Governor falls 11.2.95

We're back on our own way "home".

It was a remarkable trip with the whole group reaching the Womotoba falls then the most adventurous among the men went for the big Frederick falls which alas they failed to reach.

Altogether though this journey was a great success because the spirit was tremendous among the members of this multi-national group. You had fishermen (river and sea), hunters(?) and observers.

Champion of the fishermen became Pig who caught every night before and during before an at least one "motorcar" and another one.

The camping sites were all marvelous spots except the last one which was full with every living insects of the bush. It was there and then that I became a blood donor. This was the price to pay to the gods o' the wilderness.

Taza and his crew are remarkable people. He is the driving power behind everything and a very good organizer.

Much more is to be written, but it is better that the events of this journey are to be told to others so that will be easier to undertake such a trip under guidance, so that nature will not suffer.

Carlos

187

July, 11th 1993

Too many chiefs and no indians.
Too many doctors and no patients
Everybody has to contribute to make everybody happy
And I contribute by being a patient
Since everybody was or make believe to be happy
I think this was the perfect setting
So for the future, has more blessing

Jean,

A Most wonderful and unforgettable trip

CYRIL V. JONG

Thanks to the Surinamese team—

The guys who always made it their priority to explore new boundaries at our own expense on every venture: Dr. R.R. Lifasjoe, Roy Kong, the late Ping, Roucon Durjan and his Netherlands group, and Roy Guyadin with his military buddies.

Special gratitude to my friend Doug Meurs, a Diplomat. His advice, encouragement, adventurous zeal, and willingness to participate in several daring expeditions in the upper Corentyne Reaches have been invaluable.

---

www.ingramcontent.com/pod-product-compliance
Lightning Source LLC
Chambersburg PA
CBHW051149120626
46547CB00012B/1002